CHRONOLOGY AND DOCUMENTARY HANDBOOK OF THE STATE OF

ARKANSAS

ELLEN LLOYD TROVER,

State Editor

WILLIAM F. SWINDLER,

Series Editor

1972 OCEANA PUBLICATIONS, INC./ Dobbs Ferry, New York

This is Volume 4 in the series CHRONOLOGIES AND DOCUMENTARY
HANDBOOKS OF THE STATES.

© Copyright 1972 by Oceana Publications, Inc.

Library of Congress Cataloging in Publication Data
Main entry under title:

Chronology and documentary handbook of the State of
    Arkansas.

    (Chronologies and documentary handbooks of the States,
v. 4)
    SUMMARY: Contains a chronology of historical events
from 1541 to 1970, a directory of political figures, an
outline of the state constitution, and copies of four
historical documents.
    Bibliography: p.
    1. Arkansas--History--Chronology. 2. Arkansas--Bio-
graphy--Dictionaries. 3. Arkansas--History--Sources.
[1. Arkansas--History] I. Trover, Ellen Lloyd, ed.
II. Series.
F411.C57   976.7   72-5331
ISBN 0-379-16129-X

Manufactured in the United States of America

CONTENTS

CONTENTS

INTRODUCTION

This projected series of *Chronologies and Documentary Handbooks of the States* will ultimately comprise fifty separate volumes — one for each of the states of the Union. Each volume is intended to provide a concise ready reference of basic data on the state, and to serve as a starting point for more extended study as the individual user may require. Hopefully, it will be a guidebook for a better informed citizenry — students, civic and service organizations, professional and business personnel, and others.

The editorial plan for the *Handbook* series falls into five divisions: (1) a chronology of selected events in the history of the state; (2) a short biographical directory of the principal public officials, e.g., governors, Senators and Representatives; (3) an analytical outline of the state constitution; (4) the text of some representative documents illustrating main currents in the political, economic, social or cultural history of the state; and (5) a selected bibliography for those seeking further or more detailed information. Most of the data found in the present volume, in fact, have been taken from one or another of these references.

The user of these *Handbooks* may ask why the full text of the state constitution, or the text of constitutional documents which affected the history of the state, have not been included. There are several reasons: In the case of the current constitution, the text in almost all cases is readily available from one or more official agencies within the state. In addition, the current constitutions of all fifty states, as well as the federal Constitution, are regularly kept up to date in the definitive collection maintained by the Legislative Drafting Research Fund of Columbia University and published by the publisher of the present series of *Handbooks*. These texts are available in most major libraries under the title, *Constitutions of the United States: National and State*, in two volumes, with a companion volume, the *Index Digest of State Constitutions*.

Finally, the complete collection of documents illustrative of the constitutional development of each state, from colonial or territorial status up to the current constitution as found in the Columbia University collection, is being prepared for publication in a multi-volume series by the present series editor. Whereas the present series of *Handbooks* is intended for a wide range of interested citizens, the series of annotated constitutional materials in the volumes of *Sources and Documents of U.S. Constitutions* is primarily for the specialist in government, history or law. This is not to suggest that the general citizenry may not profit equally from referring to these materials; rather, it points up the separate purpose of the *Handbooks*, which is to guide the user to these and other sources of authoritative information with which he may systematically enrich his knowledge of this state and its place in the American Union.

William F. Swindler
Series Editor

CHRONOLOGY
1541 - 1970

CHRONOLOGY

1541	*June 18.* Hernando De Soto and his followers, the first white men to visit Arkansas, spent nearly a year in exploration.
1542	*May 21.* De Soto died at the Indian village of Guachoya, near the mouth of the Red River.
1673	Marquette and Joliet descended the Mississippi River to the mouth of the Arkansas.
	July. Marquette and Joliet arrived at the mouth of the Arkansas River and smoked the peace-pipe with the Quapaw Indians; they were the first French explorers to enter Arkansas.
1682	Le Marquis de La Salle descended the Mississippi to its mouth and claimed the entire valley for France, naming it Louisiana.
	March 12. La Salle and Henri de Tonti arrived at the mouth of Arkansas on their way to the mouth of the Mississippi.
1686	De Tonti established Arkansas Post, the first white settlement in the lower Mississippi Valley.
1719	John Law colony was established at Arkansas Post; a Scottist promoter, John Law had attempted to colonize the area with Europeans under French authority.
1721	John Law colony was abandoned, as the "Mississippi Bubble" burst; the settlers had not been properly prepared for winter in the wilderness.
1762	France ceded Louisiana to Spain, after having acquired it from Spain after La Salle's expedition at the end of the seventeenth century.
1769	Spaniards took over Louisiana, and renamed Arkansas Post, Fort Charles III.

1794   Cherokee, involved in Muscle Shoals (Tennessee)
                massacred, migrated to Arkansas.

1800   Spain returned Louisiana to France by secret treaty.

1803   *April 30*. U.S. purchased Louisiana for $15,000,000.

                William Henry Harrison became governor of the
                Indian Territory, to which the Louisiana District,
                including Arkansas, was first attached.

1804   *March 10*. Upper Louisiana was transferred to Major
                Amos Stoddard, representative of the U.S.; the
                ceremony took place at St. Louis.

                March 26. President Jefferson approved an act of
                Congress dividing Louisiana into the territories of
                Orleans and Louisiana. Arkansas was included in the
                latter.

1805   *March 3*. The territory of Louisiana (including
                Arkansas) was created by act of Congress and General
                James Wilkinson was appointed governor.

1806   *June 27*. The Territorial Legislature of Louisiana set
                off the Southern part of New Madrid District as the
                "Dictrict of Arkansas" and Stephen Worrell was
                appointed deputy governor for the district.

1807   *January 9*. Lieutenant James B. Wilkinson and party
                arrived at Arkansas Post, having descended the
                Arkansas River from Colorado in canoes. The
                lieutenant was the son of the current territorial
                governor, and the expedition may have been part of
                General Wilkinson's empire-building ambitions of this
                period.

                Meriwether Lewis was appointed governor of
                Louisiana Territory.

1808   *August 23*. The first civil officers for the District of
                Arkansas were appointed by Governor Meriwether
                Lewis.

                November 10. A treaty was negotiated with the Osage
                Indians by which a large part of Arkansas was ceded
                to the United States.

1809   Benjamin A. Howard was governor of Louisiana
                Territory.

                First census showed 1,062 population.

1811   New Madrid earthquake hit the Mississippi Valley and
                caused topographical changes in Arkansas.

1812   *May 6*. President Madison approved an act directing
                that 6,000,000 acres of land be surveyed and set
                apart as bounty lands for the soldiers of the War of
                1812. About one-third of these lands were in the
                present State of Arkansas.

                June 4. Territory of Missouri (including Arkansas)
                was created by Congress.

                December 7. The District of Arkansas was
                represented in the first legislature of the Missouri
                Territory, meeting in St. Louis.

                Benjamin A. Howard was governor of Missouri
                Territory.

1813   William Clark was governor of Missouri Territory.

                December 31. Missouri Territorial Legislature created
                Arkansas County and the county of New Madrid.
                New Madrid consisted of the lower part of Missouri
                and the upper part of Arkansas; the remainder of the
                territory was Arkansas County.

1815   *January 15.* Lawrence County created with its county seat at Davidsonville. It included 31 of the present counties of Arkansas and was named after naval Captain James Lawrence, killed in the War of 1812.

1817   *June.* Davidsonville, Lawrence County, acquired the first Arkansas post office.

July 8. A treaty was concluded with the Cherokee Indians by which the tribe ceded a portion of its lands east of the Mississippi and was granted land in Arkansas.

1818   *March 16.* Delegate John Scott of Missouri Territory presented the first petition by inhabitants of southern Missouri asking for division of the Territory.

August 24. Quapaw treaty ceded to U.S. nearly all of the land between the Arkansas and Red Rivers.

December 15. Clark,Hempstead and Pulaski counties were created at the last session of the Territorial Council. Clark was named for William Clark, Governor of the Missouri Territory; Hempstead was named for Edward Hempstead, the first delegate to Congress for the Missouri Territory; and Pulaski for Count Vladimir Pulaski, Polish hero of the American Revolution.

1819   *March 2.* Arkansas became a Territory by Congressional act approved by President Monroe. The bill had gone through much debate on slavery in the territory.

March 3. James I. Miller was appointed the first governor. He was a veteran of War of 1812 and professional soldier.

July 4. The territorial government was organized at Arkansas Post, the temporary seat of government.

1819   *July 28.* The first Territorial Legislature met at Arkansas Post. This Legislature was composed of Robert Crittenden, acting governor, Charles Jouett, Andrew Scott and Robert P. Letcher, judges.

November 20. Arkansas Gazette founded at Arkansas Post by William E. Woodruff. It was the first newspaper printed in Arkansas.

November 20. The first election was held in Arkansas for a delegate to Congress and members of the Territorial Legislature. Delegate was James W. Bates, brother of Missouri statesman Edward Bates, and territorial judge.

1820   *February 7.* The first General Assembly composed of members elected by the people, met at Arkansas Post in special session to consider the legality of the legislative council.

March. A post office was established at Little Rock, with Amos Wheeler as postmaster.

April 1. Miller County was created and named for James Miller, first territorial governor.

April 1. The steamboat "Comet" arrived at Arkansas Post. This was the first steamboat to navigate the Arkansas River.

May 1. Phillips County was created and named for Sylvanus Phillips, who settled near the mouth of the St. Francis in 1797.

October 11. The legislature approved a bill making Little Rock the capital after June 1, 1821.

October 18. General Andrew Jackson and General Thomas Hinds concluded a treaty with the Choctaw Indians, by which the tribe was granted a large tract of land in western Arkansas.

1820   *October 18.* Crawford County was created and named for William E. Crawford, Secretary of War in 1815.

October 20. Independence County was created.

The first school in Arkansas was established at Dwight Mission, near present day Russellville.

Census reported 14,273 persons in territory.

1821   *June 1.* The capital was moved from Arkansas Post to Little Rock, pursuant to an act passed at the preceding session of the Legislature.

1822   Dwight Mission, near present day Russellville, opened school for Cherokee.

March 22. The steamboat, *Eagle*, reached Little Rock, the first steamboat to ascend the Arkansas River to that point.

1823   *October 25.* Chicot County was created and named for Point Chicot on the Mississippi.

December 1. Henry W. Conway, veteran of War of 1812, seated as territorial delegate.

1824   Congress granted $15,000 for a military road from Memphis to Little Rock.

November 15. The Quapaw Indians ceded their reservation south of the Arkansas River to the U.S.

1825   George Izard was governor of Arkansas Territory until he died on November 22. He had been veteran of War of 1812.

January 20. By treaty the Chocktaw Indians ceded back to the U.S. the lands in Arkansas granted to them by the treaty of October 18, 1820. (The Calhoun Treaty).

1825   *October 20.* Conway County was created and named for Henry W. Conway, Arkansas Territorial delegate to Congress.

October 20. Izard County was created and named for Governor George Izard.

October 22. Crittenden County was created and named for Robert Crittenden, first secretary of the Arkansas Territory.

1826   *July 27.* First steam sawmill in Arkansas began operations at Helena.

1827   *October 13.* Lovely County was created and abolished on October 28, 1828.

October 15. Lafayette County was created and named for the Marquis de La Fayette.

October 27. St. Francis County was created and named for the river through it.

1828   *May 6.* Cherokee by treaty agreed to leave Arkansas; the present western boundary was established.

October 17. Sevier County was formed and named for Ambrose H. Sevier, speaker of the House of Representatives, who had just been elected territorial delegate.

October 17. Washington County was created and named for George Washington.

1829   *January 6.* President John Quincy Adams approved an act giving to the people of Arkansas the privilege of electing their county officers.

January 7. Acting-Governor Crittenden issued a proclamation ordering settlers to be moved from the Indian lands. The order caused much dissatisfaction.

1829   *November 2.* Jefferson, Hot Spring, Monroe, Pope,
            and Union counties were created; Hot Springs was
            named for the hot springs within its boundaries;
            Jefferson was named for Thomas Jefferson, Monroe
            for James Monroe; Pope for Governor John Pope; and
            Union for the United States.

            November 5. Jackson County was created and named
            for President Andrew Jackson.

            John Pope was governor. A prominent Kentucky
            political leader, he served as U.S. Senator there
            both before and after his territorial office.

1830   Census: 30,388.

1831   *March 2.* President Jackson approved the act granting
            to the Territory of Arkansas ten sections of land for
            the erection of public buildings.

            November 7. Little Rock was incorporated as a town
            by act of the Legislature.

1832   *June 15.* President Jackson approved an act granting
            to the territory of Arkansas 1,000 acres of land for
            the erection of a courthouse and jail.

1833   *November 1.* Carroll, Mississippi and Pike Counties
            were created; Carroll was named for Charles Carroll
            of Maryland, one of the signers of the Declaration of
            Independence; Mississippi was named for the river;
            and Pike was named for Lieutenant Zebulon M. Pike,
            the explorer.

            November 5. Greene and Scott counties were created;
            Greene was named for Nathaniel Greene,
            Revolutionary War General; and Scott for Andrew
            Scott, judge of the Superior Court of the Arkansas
            Territory.

1833   *November 11.* Van Buren County was created and named in honor of Vice President Martin Van Buren.

November 16. Johnson County was created and named for Judge Benjamin Johnson.

December 17. Delegate Sevier proposed a resolution in the House of Representatives that the Committee on Territories inquire into a constitutional convention for Arkansas pending statehood.

1835   William Fulton was governor. He had been territorial secretary and a territorial judge.

October 23. White County was created and named for Hugh L. White of Tennessee, a Whig candidate for president.

October 29. Randolph County was created and named for John Randolph of Virginia.

November 2. Saline County was created and named Saline because of the salt works; De Soto had called the area Provincia de la Sal (Province of Salt).

November 2. Little Rock was incorporated as a city.

November 3. Marion County was created and named to honor Francis Marion, the Revolutionary War General (its original name was Searcy County with the change in 1836).

December 8. An election was held for delegates to a Constitutional Convention.

1836   *January 4.* The first constitutional convention met in the Baptist Church in Little Rock.

June 15. Arkansas admitted to the Union as the 25th State when President Jackson approved the bill.

1836   *September 12.* The first State Legislature met at Little Rock.

September 13. James Sevier Conway became the first governor of state. A member of prominent Tennessee and Arkansas family, he had been surveyor general of territory.

September 30. Benton and Madison counties were created. Benton was named for Thomas H. Benton, Senator from Missouri, and Madison after Madison County, Alabama.

November 2. The State Bank of Arkansas was incorporated by act of the legislature.

December 13. Searcy County was created and named for Richard Searcy, territorial judge.

1837   *September 4.* Ambrose Sevier and ex-Governor Fulton seated as first U.S. Senators. First Representative was Archibald Yell, territorial judge.

December 19. Franklin County was created and named in honor of Benjamin Franklin.

1838   *February 28.* Poinsett County was created and named for J. Roberts Poinsett, Secretary of War.

December 12. Desha County was created and named for Captain Benjamin Desha of the War of 1812 who came to settle in Arkansas in 1822.

The first revised code of Arkansas law was published.

1839   *June 27.* The first steam ferry on the Arkansas River was established at Little Rock.

December 2. Judge Edward Cross seated as U.S. Representative.

1840   Archibald Yell was governor.

December 5. Yell County was created and named for Governor Archibald Yell.

December 14. Perry County was created and named for Commodore Oliver Hazard Perry, hero of the battle of Lake Erie in the War of 1812.

December 18. Bradley County was created and named for Captain Hugh Bradley who served with General Jackson and settled in the area in 1821.

Census: 97,574 persons.

1842   *November 29.* Ouachita County was created and named for the river that bisects the county.

December 9. Montgomery County was created and named for General Richard Montgomery of the Revolution.

December 14. Newton County was created and named for Thomas W. Newton of Arkansas.

December 21. Fulton County was created and named for William S. Fulton, last governor of the Arkansas Territory.

December 24. Fort Smith was incorporated as a city by act of the Legislature.

1843   *December 4.* Chester Ashley, leader of state bar, elected to seat of Senator Fulton, deceased.

1844   *April 29.* Governor Yell resigned to run for Congress; he was succeeded by Samuel Adams, president of the Senate.

Thomas S. Drew was governor. A planter and member of constitutional convention, Drew was member of

1844   Tennessee migration which dominated early state
               politics.

               November 30. Polk County was created and named
               for President James K. Polk.

1845   *January 1*. Dallas County was created and named in
               honor of George M. Dallas, Vice President of the
               United States.

1846   *July 30*. The Arkansas penitentiary was destroyed by
               fire started by one of the convicts.

               October 25. Prairie County was created and named
               for the Grand Prairie.

               December 26. Drew County was created and named
               for Governor Thomas S. Drew.

1847   *February 6*. Thomas W. Newton, banker, elected to
               seat of Congressman Yell, who had accepted Army
               commission in Mexican War.

               December 6. Robert W. Johnson, state attorney
               general, seated as U.S. Representative.

1848   *November 30*. Ashley County was created and named
               for Chester Ashley, Senator from Arkansas.

               December 4. Senator Sevier resigned and Senator
               Ashley died. Two new Senators were Solon Borland,
               a physician, and Supreme Court Justice William K.
               Sebastian.

1849   *January 10*. Governor Drew resigned and was
               succeeded by Richard C. Byrd, president of the
               Senate.

               John S. Roane, speaker of state lower house and
               prominent attorney, elected governor.

1850   *December 6.* Calhoun County was created and named for John C. Calhoun.

Census: 209,897 population.

1851   *January 6.* Sebastian County was created and named for U.S. Senator William K. Sebastian.

1852   *December 17.* Columbia County was created.

Cane Hill College received its charter.

Elias N. Conway, brother of former governor James S. Conway, elected governor.

1853   *January 10.* Legislature granted the first railroad charter to the Arkansas Central Railroad Company.

February 9. Congress granted to the Cairo and Fulton Railroad Company each alternate section of land along the proposed route, for a certain distance each side of the right of way.

December 5. Senator Borland having been appointed minister to Central America, Congressman Johnson was elected to his seat. New Representatives were Alfred B. Greenwood, attorney and jurist, and Edward A. Warren, veteran legislator.

1855   *December 3.* Congressman Warren succeeded by Albert Rust, another state legislative veteran.

1857   *December 7.* Congressman Warren regained seat lost to Congressman Rust.

1858   Butterfield Stage Lines (St. Louis-California) operated through northwest Arkansas.

The Memphis and Little Rock railroad began operating trains between Hopefield on the Mississippi and Madison on the St. Francis River.

1859   *February 19.* Craighead County was created and
              named for Thomas B. Craighead, State Senator.

              March 4. Governor Elias N. Conway approved an act
              of the Legislature incorporating the school for the
              blind at Arkadelphia.

              December 5. New Congressmen: Albert Rust and
              Thomas C. Hindman, Mexican War veteran and
              former leader of Mississippi legislature.

1860   Telegraph line opened between St. Louis and
              Fayetteville.

              August. Judge Henry M. Rector was elected governor.

              December 5. The Democratic state convention, which
              met at Little Rock, declared that Congress could not
              impair the right of citizens to hold slaves.

              Census: 435,450 population.

1861   *January 1.* The Legislature passed an act for the
              incorporation of the first cotton seed oil mill, at Pine
              Bluff.

              January 15. The governor signed a law calling for a
              vote on secession.

              March 4. The convention on secession met in Little
              Rock.

              May 6. The state convention adopted a secession
              ordinance by a vote of 69 to 1.

              May 18. Arkansas was admitted to the Confederacy
              by unanimous vote by the states.

              July 11. Congressional delegation resigned.

1861   *November 4.* A special session of the legislature met
            for two weeks to provide for the payment of the
            Confederate War tax.

1862   *March 17-22.* A session of the legislature met and
            authorized the governor to move the capital.

            March. The legislature prohibited the distillation of
            any kind of grain or potatoes into liquors for the
            duration of the war in order to promote saving food.

            The legislature imposed a tax of $30 a bale on cotton
            to encourage the planting of food.

            May 1. The legislature passed the "twenty nigger"
            law, exempting one white man from military service
            on every plantation having 20 negroes or more.

            June 2. Governor Rector issued a proclamation
            transferring all Arkansas troops to the service of the
            Confederacy.

            June 30. General Hindman declared the state to be
            under martial law due to the ineffectiveness of the
            civil authorities.

            July 19. John S. Phelps of Missouri was appointed
            military governor by Lincoln.

            July 30. General T. H. Holmes was sent to Arkansas
            to relieve Hindman of command.

            August 12. General Holmes established his
            headquarters at Little Rock but left Hindman in
            command of the field.

            October. Colonel Harris Flanagin of Clark county was
            elected governor.

            November 4. Governor Rector resigned although his
            term was not to expire until November 15. Thomas

1862   Fletcher of Arkansas County, president of the Senate, became acting governor.

November 15. Cross County was created and named for Colonel David Cross, the first colonel of the Fifth Arkansas Infantry of the Confederacy.

November 26. Woodruff County was created and named for William E. Woodruff, founder of the *Arkansas Gazette.*

1863   *January 11.* Arkansas Post was captured by the Federal forces under General McClernand.

January 29. Jefferson Davis suspended the writ of habeas corpus in Arkansas and the Indian county but admonished Holmes to abstain from control of persons and property except where necessary for defense and military discipline.

May 1. The "twenty nigger" law was modified to cover only the plantation of minors, dependents, and men in the service.

July 9. Phelp's commission was revoked.

September. Governor Harris Flanagin ordered the seat of government to be removed from Little Rock to Washington, Hempstead County.

September 10. Little Rock fell to federal forces under General Frederick Steele.

1864   *January 4.* The Unionist constitutional convention assembled in Little Rock. It adopted a constitution and adjourned on the 23rd.

March 14. Judges of the Supreme and circuit courts were elected.

1864

April 18. Isaac Murphy was inaugurated Unionist governor. An army veteran from Pennsylvania, Murphy's policy aimed at speedy restoration of Arkansas to Union.

May 23. An act was passed authorizing county courts to sit at any place they might consider safe for the court and the records, and directing county clerks to follow the courts.

May 28. An act passed which prohibited the collection of taxes on realty except that belonging to persons in arms against the U.S. or Arkansas, or who had aided the rebellion.

May 31. A general revenue act was passed which suspended all corporate powers of cities and towns until January 1, 1865.

A stay law was enacted; it suspended the collection of all debts contracted prior to January 1, 1864, except debts of persons who had not taken the oath of allegiance or had taken the oath and violated it.

An act was passed for the regulation of elections; it required each voter to take an oath to support the U.S. Constitution.

1865

April 13. The legislature ratified the 13th amendment.

May 24. The last military action of the Civil War in Arkansas occurred, a skirmish near Monticello.

May 26. The Confederate government in Arkansas came to an end.

June 19. The restrictions on trade were announced to be raised by General J.J. Reynolds.

1865   *September 30.* The Arkansas Immigration Aid
             Society was organized to encourage white settlers
             from the North.

1866   *December. Hawkins v. Filkins*, the Supreme Court
             held the state government, except in its allegiance to
             the U.S., was not affected by the ordinance of session
             and "that the ordinance of the convention of 1864
             made void the action of the convention of 1861 only
             so far as the same" was in conflict with the
             constitution and laws of the United States.

1867   *March 5.* Little River County was created and named
             for the river forming part of its boundary.

1868   *January 7 - February 14.* The fourth Arkansas
             Constitutional Convention met at Little Rock.

             July 18. Sharp County was created and named for
             Ephraim Sharp, legislator.

             June 22. Arkansas was readmitted to the Union. New
             Congressional delegation included Senators Alexander
             McDonald, banker, and Benjamin F. Rice, attorney.
             Representatives: Logan H. Roots, planter, James
             Hinds, attorney, James T. Elliott, former judge, and
             Thomas Boles, Confederate veteran. All but Elliott
             were Republicans.

             July 2. Powell Clayton, the first reconstructionist
             governor under the Constitution of 1868, was
             inaugurated. An army engineer and planter, Clayton
             undertook stronger program of federal control.

             November 4. Governor Clayton issued a proclamation
             declaring martial law in 13 counties.

1869   *February 4.* An act was approved authorizing any
             incorporated city or town to form a separate school
             district.

1869   *February 4*. Grant County was created and named for President Ulysses S. Grant.

              March 4. Anthony A. C. Rogers, businessman and Union Democrat, elected to Congress.

              April 9. Boone County was created; the original name was "Boon" as it was supposed to be a "boon" to the residents to give them a closer county seat.

              June 19. The Arkansas River Valley Immigration Company was organized by lower Arkansas valley planters to bring Chinese laborers into the state.

1870   Census: 484,471 persons.

1871   *March 17*. Governor Clayton resigned to become U.S. Senator succeeding Senator McDonald. O.A. Hadley, local businessman, became acting governor. New Congressmen: James N. Hanks, former judge, and Oliver P. Snyder, leader of post war constitutional convention.

              March 20. Nevada County was created and named for the state of Nevada because their outlines are similar.

              March 22. Logan County was created; its original name was Saber for the State Senator; the change honored James Logan, an early pioneer.

              March 27. The University of Arkansas was established by act of the Legislature under the Morrill Act and was named the Arkansas Industrial University.

              March 28. Lincoln County was created and named for Abraham Lincoln.

              April 11. Railroad from Little Rock to Memphis completed.

1872   *January 22.* Arkansas Industrial University (now University of Arkansas) opened at Fayettesville with 8 students.

1873   *January 3.* Elisha Baxter was elected governor, in what was regarded end of Reconstruction. Challenge by "carpetbaggers" next year led to local "civil war." Democrats won back several Congressional seats.

March 24. Baxter and Clay counties were created; Baxter was named for Governor Elisha Baxter and Clay for John M. Clayton, member of the State Senate.

April 5. Garland County was created and named for Augustus H. Garland, state leader in restoration of civil rights for former Confederates.

April 12. Faulkner County was created and named for Colonel Sanford C. Faulkner, credited with being the original Arkansas Traveller.

April 16. Lonoke County was created, the name is said to come from "Lone Oak".

April 17. Dorsey and Lee counties were created; in 1885, the name of Dorsey was changed to Cleveland to honor Grover Cleveland, and Lee was named to honor General Robert E. Lee.

April 17. Howard County was created and named for James Howard, State Senator.

April 21. Stone County was created and named for the geological structure of the region.

The first bridge across the Arkansas (Barine Cross) completed.

1874   *April 15.* Joseph Brooks, claiming to have been elected governor and armed with a decision of the

1874   Pulaski County Circuit Court, went to the State House and ejected Governor Elisha Baxter. This was the beginning of the Brooks-Baxter War.

May 15. President Grant issued a proclamation recognizing Elisha Baxter as governor.

July 14-September 7. The fifth Constitutional Convention met at Little Rock.

October 13. The new constitution was ratified by popular vote and state officers were elected.

Augustus H. Garland was elected governor. Formerly state auditor, his administration undertook to liquidate large postwar state debt.

October 15. Governor Garland elected U.S. Senator.

1879   *July 1.* The U.S. Weather Bureau at Little Rock was opened.

December. James D. Walker elected to Senate, restoring Congressional delegation to Democrats.

1880   Census: 802,525 persons.

1881   Thomas J. Churchill became governor. He was leading planter and businessman.

1882   *March 15.* The Arkansas State Bar Association was organized at Little Rock.

1883   *February 20.* Cleburne County was created and named for Patrick R. Cleburne, Arkansas major-general in the Confederate Army.

James H. Berry, attorney and Confederate veteran, became governor.

1885   Simon P. Hughes, formerly of state supreme court, became governor.

           Senator Garland named Attorney General of United States under Grover Cleveland. Governor Berry succeeded to Garland's seat.

1889   James P. Eagle, clergyman and planter, elected governor.

1890   Census: 1,128,211 population.

1892   Poll tax made prerequisite for voting.

1893   William M. Fishback, attorney and leader in constitutional revision, became governor.

           Convict leasing system abolished.

1894   *October 2*. A destructive tornado struck Little Rock causing over one million dollars damage. Two persons were killed and 40 injured.

1895   James P. Clarke, legislative veteran, elected governor.

1897   Daniel W. Jones, former attorney general of state, became governor.

1898   *January 11*. A tornado at Fort Smith destroyed $1,000,000 worth of property and killed over 50 people.

1900   Census: 1,311,564.

1901   Jeff Davis, state attorney general and later U.S. Senator, elected governor.

1904   Arkansas Supreme Court invalidated the poll tax amendment.

1906   *August 1*. Diamonds were discovered in Pike County by John M. Huddleston.

1907   Judge John S. Little elected governor.

        February 11. Due to ill health Governor Little vacated his office and was succeeded by John I. Moore, president of the Senate, who served until May 14, 1907. X.O. Pindall, president pro tempore of the Senate, succeeded Moore and served until January 14, 1909.

1908   Poll tax amendment readopted.

1909   George W. Donaghey, businessman and engineer, elected governor.

1910   Census: 1,574,449.

1911   Legislature met in the new Capital.

1913   State Highway Department established.

        January. Joe T. Robinson, former Congressman and future Senator, elected governor.

        March 10. Joe Robinson resigned and was succeeded by W.K. Oldham, president of the Senate. Three days later, when the legislature adjourned, Oldham was succeeded by J.M. Futrell, who served until July 23, 1913.

        February 21. The Arkansas Legislature ratified the amendment to the U.S. Constitution authorizing the election of senators by direct vote.

        February 26. The official flag was adopted.

        George W. Hays, clergyman and educator, elected governor.

1915   Child labor law and women's minimum
            wage-and-hour act passed.

1916   *January 1.* Statewide prohibition began.

1917   Charles H. Brough, another educator, became
            governor.

            Compulsory education adopted.

            Camp Pike built near Little Rock.

            November 19. A constitutional convention met at
            Little Rock.

1918   Women admitted to Democratic primaries.

            December 14. The new constitution was rejected by
            the voters - 37,184 to 23,280.

1920   Oil discovered in Ouachita and Union Counties.

            Census: 1,752,204.

1921   Thomas C. McRae, attorney and business leader,
            became governor.

1923   Act providing for State Tuberculosis Sanatorium for
            Negroes passed.

            The state highway system was created by the General
            Assembly.

1924   Remmel Dam, first major hydroelectric development,
            created.

1925   Tom J. Terral, former secretary of state, became
            governor.

            Arkansas was the first state to ratify Federal Child
            Labor Amendment.

1926   The office of Lieutenant-Governor was established.

1927   *January*. John E. Martineau was governor; Governor Martineau resigned to accept appointment to an Arkansas Federal judgeship, on March 4, 1928. Harvey Parnell, the state's first elected lieutenant governor, succeeded as governor.

            The Martineau Road Law was enacted to provide for a uniform system of improved highway.

            The greatest flood in state history covered one-fifth of Arkansas' land.

1928   Harvey Parnell, state business leader, became governor.

            The teaching of evolution was prohibited.

1929   Act passed providing $3,250,000 for new State Hospital for Nervous Diseases, located near Benton.

1930   Census: 1,854,482.

1932   *November 9*. Hattie W. Carraway, the first woman to U.S. Senate, elected for a full term.

1933   J.M. Futrell became governor.

            July 18. Statewide prohibition was repealed.

1934   *November*. Governor Futrell was re-elected.

1935   The sales tax was first enacted.

1937   Carl E. Bailey, state attorney general, became governor.

1940   *June*. The U.S. Supreme Court ruled against Arkansas in the boundary dispute with Tennessee.

1940   *October*. The Arkansas Supreme Court barred the
                Communist party from the election ballot.

                Census: 1,949,387.

1941   Homer M. Adkins was elected governor.

1942   *July*. The Arkansas Negro Democratic Association
                president, Dr. J.M. Robinson, advised Negroes to vote
                in primary elections despite party bans.

1944   *July*. State Democratic Committee amended the
                party rules to permit primary officials to challenge
                Negroes on party loyalty grounds.

                September. The Democratic convention amended
                party rules to allow Negroes to vote in primaries.

                November. The voters approved constitutional
                amendments opposing closed shop union contracts
                and removing poll tax as a prerequisite for men and
                women in the service.

1945   Ben T. Laney was elected governor.

1946   *November*. Governor Laney was re-elected.

1947   *January*. The Legislature adopted a measure repealing
                the 1945 separation of State and Federal primaries
                which was designed to keep Negroes from voting.

1948   *November*. The voters approved a Constitutional
                amendment authorizing the Legislature to institute a
                registration system as a voting requirement.

1949   Sid McMath was elected governor.

                February. Arkansas University was honored by the
                Negro Newspaper Publishers Association for 1948
                student admissions.

1950   *September*. The Democratic State Convention
                approved opening of Democratic primaries to Negroes
                and permitted them to qualify as candidates.

                Census: 1,909,511.

1952   *November*. Judge Francis Cherry was elected
                governor.

                November. The voters rejected a plan for a 1%
                property tax to promote new industry.

1954   *November*. Orval E. Faubus was elected governor.

1956   *November*. Governor Faubus was re-elected.

1957   *February*. Governor Faubus signed anti-integration
                bills.

                August. Federal District Court ordered integration of
                high schools. Chancery court granted the Mothers
                League plea for a temporary injunction. Federal
                Judge Davis declared the injunction void.

                September. Governor Faubus ordered the National
                Guard and Arkansas State police to Central High
                School, Little Rock, to prevent violence.

                September. Judge Davis ordered the U.S. to seek an
                injunction to end Governor Faubus' interference with
                integration of Little Rock high schools.

1958   *March*. The Arkansas Supreme Court, 4-3, declined to
                pass on whether Eisenhower acted within his
                authority in ordering troops.

                July. Faubus re-elected governor by landslide; he was
                the first to win a third term since 1904.

                August. Governor Faubus urged the Legislature to
                back a policy of non-surrender to the Federal

1958

Government; he recommended a program giving him powers to close any public school integrated by force.

September 12. The U.S. Supreme Court rejected the Little Rock School Board appeal for an integration delay and made the ruling effective immediately because of imminence of the new school year.

September. Faubus signed bills giving him wide powers over the educational system, including the right to close schools; he ordered all high schools in Little Rock closed.

1959

January. Governor Faubus proposed a constitutional amendment and law to let students collect tuition payments rather than attend the public school system.

January. The Legislature approved the Faubus anti-integration proposal, including the bill permitting direct payment of public funds to students for use at schools of their choice.

March. A three judge Federal District Court barred further diversion of state funds from closed high school system to other public and private institutions.

April. The Arkansas Supreme Court, 4-3, ruled the Legislature did not exceed its police powers by ordering the closing of the public school system.

June. A Federal Court held the Arkansas school-closing law unconstitutional and invalidated the act providing funds to pupils transferring to other schools.

December. The U.S. Supreme Court held unconstitutional the Arkansas laws which Faubus used to close the high school system.

1960   Orval Faubus was re-elected governor.

      Census: 1,786,272.

1961   *January*. Governor Faubus proposed a Constitutional amendment to let pupils get a public education even though they refuse to attend desegregated schools. The Legislature approved.

      July. Four counties received first Federal loans under the depressed areas bill.

      August. Representatives Butler and Pryor campaigned for a new Constitution.

1962   *March*. A Negro was named Employment Security Division section head, the highest post ever held by a Negro in the state.

      November. Governor Faubus was re-elected.

1964   *November 3*. Governor Faubus defeated Winthrop Rockefeller in gubernatorial race.

1965   *March 1*. All 715,528 voters were disqualified as a result of the confusion over the Constitutional amendment that abolished the poll tax and set up the PPR system; the amendment stipulated that voter lists based on poll-tax payments could be used only until March 1, and legal disputes have kept the state from printing new registration forms.

      March. State police removed from the Capitol building 25 demonstrators seeking to integrate the Capitol Cafeteria.

      November. A three judge Federal Court approved the Legislature's reapportionment plan to be put into effect by the November 1966 elections.

1966   *November*. Winthrop Rockefeller defeated Justice
              Johnson, a strong segregationist, for governor.

1967   *January*. Rockefeller was sworn in as the first
              Republican Governor since Reconstruction.

              May. Attorney General Purcell held it was illegal for
              Rockefeller to supplement employees' pay out of his
              own pocket.

1969   *June*. A constitutional convention opened in Little
              Rock; it was the first in 51 years.

              July. A. U.S. grand jury indicted 15 former prison
              officials and guards on charges of performing brutal
              acts against inmates at Tucker and Cummins State
              Farms and at 2 county penal farms.

1970   *October*. The Arkansas Supreme Court ruled
              unconstitutional the law providing for run-off
              elections for state offices in a suit by Republican
              members of the State Election Committee charging
              the Legislature had no power to alter constitutional
              provisions for conducting elections.

              November 3. Democrat Bumpers defeated Winthrop
              Rockefeller's bid for re-election as governor.

              November. Mississippi asked the U.S. Supreme Court
              to settle the border dispute with Arkansas over a
              stretch of the river near Greenville, concerning
              navigation channels dug in 1933 which altered flow.

              Census: 1,923,295.

BIOGRAPHICAL DIRECTORY

(Names of persons still living, or persons for whom information was incomplete, have been omitted)

ADAMS, Samuel
  b. June 5, 1805, Halifax County, Va.
  d. Feb. 27, 1850, Little Rock, Ark.
  Acting governor, 1844
ADKINS, Homer M.
  b. Oct. 15, 1890, Jacksonville, Ark.
  d. Feb. 28, 1964, Little Rock, Ark.
  Governor, 1941-45
ASHLEY, Chester
  b. June 1, 1790, Westfield, Mass.
  d. Apr. 29, 1848, Washington, D. C.
  U. S. Senator, 1844-48
BAILEY, Carl E.
  b. Oct. 8, 1894, Bernie, Me.
  d. Oct. 23, 1948, Little Rock, Ark.
  Governor, 1937-41
BATES, James W.
  b. Aug. 25, 1788, Goochland County, Va.
  d. Dec. 26, 1846, Van Buren, Ark.
  Territorial delegate, 1820-23
BAXTER, Elisha
  b. Sept. 1, 1827, Rutherford County, N. C.
  d. May 31, 1899, Little Rock, Ark.
  Governor, 1873-74
BERRY, James H.
  b. May 15, 1841, Jackson County, Ala.
  d. Jan. 30, 1913, Bentonville, Ark.
  Governor, 1883-85
  U. S. Senator, 1885-1907
BOLES, Thomas
  b. July 16, 1837, Johnson County, Ark.
  d. Mar. 13, 1905, Ft. Smith, Ark.
  U. S. Representative, 1868-71, 1872-73

31

BORLAND, Solon
  b. Sept. 21, 1808, Suffolk, Va.
  d. Jan. 1, 1864, Houston, Tex.
  U. S. Senator, 1848-53
  U. S. Minister to Nicaragua, 1853-54
BRECKINRIDGE, Clifton R.
  b. Nov. 22, 1846, Lexington, Ky.
  d. Dec. 5, 1932, Wendover, Ky.
  U. S. Representative, 1893-94
BROUGH, Charles H.
  b. July 9, 1876, Clinton, Miss.
  d. Dec. 26, 1935, Washington, D. C.
  Governor, 1917-21
BRUNDIDGE, Stephen
  b. Jan. 1, 1857, Searcy, Ark.
  d. Jan. 14, 1938, Searcy, Ark.
  U. S. Representative, 1897-1909
CARAWAY, Hattie W.
  b. Feb. 1, 1878, Bakerville, Tenn.
  d. Dec. 21, 1950, Falls Church, Va.
  U. S. Senator, 1931-45
CARAWAY, Thaddeus
  b. Oct. 17, 1871, Stoddard County, Mo.
  d. Nov. 6, 1931, Little Rock, Ark.
  U. S. Representative, 1913-21
  U. S. Senator, 1921-31
CATE, William H.
  b. Nov. 11, 1839, Rutherford County, Tenn.
  d. Aug. 23, 1899, Toledo, O.
  U. S. Representative, 1889-90, 1891-93
CHURCHILL, Thomas J.
  b. Mar. 10, 1824, Louisville, Ky.
  d. 1905, Little Rock, Ark.
  Governor, 1881-83
CLARK, William
  b. Aug. 1, 1770, Caroline County, Va.
  d. Sept. 1, 1838, St. Louis, Mo.
  Territorial governor (Missouri Terr.), 1813-15

CLARKE, James P.
  b. Aug. 18, 1854, Yazoo County, Miss.
  d. Oct. 1, 1916, Little Rock, Ark.
  Governor, 1895-97
  U. S. Senator, 1903-16
CLAYTON, Powell
  b. Aug. 7, 1833, Bethel, Pa.
  d. Aug. 25, 1914, Washington, D. C.
  Governor, 1868-71
  U. S. Senator, 1871-77
CONWAY, Elias A.
  b. Mar. 17, 1812, Greene County, Tenn.
  d. Feb. 28, 1894, Little Rock, Ark.
  Governor, 1852-60
CONWAY, Henry W.
  b. Mar. 18, 1793, Greene County, Tenn.
  d. Nov. 9, 1827, Arkansas Post, Ark.
  Territorial delegate, 1823-27
CONWAY, James Sevier
  b. Dec. 9, 1798, Greene County, Tenn.
  d. Mar. 3, 1855, Lafayette County, Ark.
  Governor, 1836-40
CRAVENS, Jordan E.
  b. Nov. 7, 1830, Fredericktown, Mo.
  d. Apr. 8, 1914, Ft. Smith, Ark.
  U. S. Representative, 1877-83
CRAVENS, William B.
  b. Jan. 17, 1872, Ft. Smith, Ark.
  d. Jan. 13, 1939, Washington, D. C.
  U. S. Representative, 1907-13, 1933-39
CROSS, Edward
  b. Nov. 11, 1798, Hawkins City, Tenn.
  d. Apr. 6, 1887, Hempstead County, Ark.
  U. S. Representative, 1829-45
DAVIS, Jeff
  b. May 6, 1862, Richmond, Ark.
  d. Jan. 3, 1913, Little Rock, Ark.
  Governor, 1901-07
  U. S. Senator, 1907-13

DINSMORE, Hugh A.
  b. Dec. 24, 1850, Benton County, Ark.
  d. May 2, 1930, St. Louis, Mo.
  U. S. Representative, 1893-05
DONAGHEY, George W.
  b. July 1, 1856, Union Parish, La.
  d. Dec. 15, 1937, Little Rock, Ark.
  Governor, 1909-13
DORSEY, Stephen W.
  b. Feb. 28, 1842, Benson, Vt.
  d. Mar. 20, 1916, Los Angeles, Calif.
  U. S. Senator, 1873-79
DREW, Thomas S.
  b. Aug. 25, 1802, Wilson County, Tenn.
  d. Apr. 17, 1867, Pine Bluff, Ark.
  Governor, 1844-49
DRIVER, William J.
  b. Mar. 2, 1873, Mississippi County, Ark.
  d. Oct. 1, 1948, Osceola, Ark.
  U. S. Representative, 1921-39
DUNN, Poindexter
  b. Nov. 3, 1834, Raleigh, N. C.
  d. Oct. 12, 1914, Texarkana, Tx.
  U. S. Representative, 1879-89
EAGLE, James P.
  b. Aug. 10, 1837, Maury County, Tenn.
  d. 1904, Little Rock, Ark.
  Governor, 1889-93
EDWARDS, John
  b. Oct. 4, 1805, Louisville, Ky.
  d. Apr. 8, 1894, Washington, D. C.
  U. S. Representative, 1871-72
ELLIOTT, James T.
  b. Apr. 22, 1823, Columbus, Ga.
  d. July 28, 1875, Camden, Ark.
  U. S. Representative, 1869
FEATHERSTONE, Lewis P.
  b. July 28, 1851, Oxford, Miss.
  d. Mar. 14, 1922, Longview, Tex.
  U. S. Representative, 1890-91

FISHBACK, William M.
  b. Nov. 5, 1831, Jeffersonton, Va.
  d. 1903, Ft. Smith, Ark.
  Governor, 1893-95
FLANAGIN, Harris
  b. Nov. 3, 1817, Roadstown, N. J.
  d. Oct. 23, 1874, Arkadelphia, Ark.
  Governor, 1862-64
FLETCHER, Thomas
  b. Apr. 8, 1819, Randolph County, Ark.
  d. Feb. 21, 1900, Little Rock, Ark.
  Governor, 1862
FLOYD, John C.
  b. Apr. 14, 1858, Sparta, Tenn.
  d. Nov. 4, 1930, Yellville, Ark.
  U. S. Representative, 1905-15
FULLER, Claude A.
  b. Jan. 20, 1876, Prophetstown, Ill.
  d. Jan. 8, 1968, Eureka Spgs., Ark.
  U. S. Representative, 1929-39
FULTON, William S.
  b. June 2, 1795, Cecil County, Md.
  d. Aug. 15, 1844, Little Rock, Ark.
  Territorial governor, 1835-36
  U. S. Senator, 1837-44
GARLAND, Augustus H.
  b. June 11, 1832, Tipton County, Tenn.
  d. Jan. 26, 1899, Washington, D. C.
  Governor, 1874-77
  U. S. Senator, 1877-85
  U. S. Attorney General, 1885-89
GAUSE, Lucien C.
  b. Dec. 25, 1836, Brunswick County, N. C.
  d. Nov. 5, 1880, Jacksonport, Ark.
  U. S. Representative, 1875-79
GLOVER, David G.
  b. Jan. 18, 1868, Prattsville, Ark.
  d. Apr. 5, 1952, Malvern, Ark.
  U. S. Representative, 1929-35

GOODWIN, William S.
  b. May 2, 1866, Warren, Ark.
  d. Aug. 9, 1937, Warren, Ark.
  U. S. Representative, 1911-21
GREENWOOD, Alfred B.
  b. July 11, 1811, Franklin County, Ga.
  d. Oct. 4, 1889, Bentonville, Ark.
  U. S. Representative, 1853-59
GUNTER, Thomas M.
  b. Sept. 18, 1826, Warren County, Tenn.
  d. Jan. 12, 1904, Fayetteville, Ark.
  U. S. Representative, 1874-83
HADLEY, Ozro A.
  b. June 30, 1826, Chautauqua County, N. Y.
  d. 1885 in New Mexico
  Acting governor, 1871-73
HANKS, James M.
  b. Feb. 12, 1833, Helena, Ark.
  d. May 24, 1909, Helena, Ark.
  U. S. Representative, 1871-73
HARRISON, William Henry
  b. Feb. 9, 1773, Charles City County, Va.
  d. Apr. 4, 1841, Washington, D. C.
  Territorial governor (Louisiana District), 1803-05
HAYS, George W.
  b. Sept. 23, 1863, Ouachita County, Ark.
  d. Sept. 15, 1927, Little Rock, Ark.
  Governor, 1913-17
HINDMAN, Thomas C.
  b. Jan. 28, 1828, Knoxville, Tenn.
  d. Sept. 27, 1868, Helena, Ark.
  U. S. Representative, 1859-61
HINDS, James
  b. Dec. 5, 1833, Hebron, N. Y.
  d. Oct. 22, 1868, Indian Bay, Ark.
  U. S. Representative, 1868

HODGES, Asa
  b. Jan. 22, 1822, Lawrence County, Ala.
  d. June 6, 1900, Marion, Ark.
  U. S. Representative, 1874-75
HOWARD, Benjamin A.
  b. 1760 in Virginia
  d. Sept. 18, 1814, St. Louis, Mo.
  Territorial governor (Louisiana Dist.), 1812-13
HUGHES, Simon P.
  b. Aug. 14, 1830, Carthage, Tenn.
  d. 1906, Little Rock, Ark.
  Governor, 1885-89
HYNES, William J.
  b. Mar. 31, 1843, County Clare, Ireland
  d. Apr. 2, 1915, Los Angeles, Calif.
  U. S. Representative, 1873-77
IZARD, George
  b. Oct. 21, 1776, in England
  d. Nov. 22, 1825, Little Rock, Ark.
  Territorial governor, 1825
JACOWAY, Henderson M.
  b. Nov. 7, 1870, Dardanelle, Ark.
  d. Aug. 4, 1947, Little Rock, Ark.
  U. S. Representative, 1911-23
JOHNSON, Robert W.
  b. July 22, 1814, Scott County, Ky.
  d. July 26, 1879, Little Rock, Ark.
  U. S. Representative, 1848-53
  U. S. Senator, 1853-61
JONES, Daniel W.
  b. Dec. 15, 1839, Republic of Texas
  d. Dec. 25, 1918, Little Rock, Ark.
  Governor, 1897-1901
JONES, James K.
  b. Sept. 29, 1839, Marshall County, Miss.
  d. June 1, 1908, Washington, D. C.
  U. S. Representative, 1881-85
  U. S. Senator, 1885-1903

KAVANAUGH, William M.
  b. Mar. 3, 1866, Greene County, Ala.
  d. Feb. 21, 1915, Little Rock, Ark.
  U. S. Senator, 1911-13
KIRBY, William F.
  b. Nov. 16, 1867, Texarkana, Ark.
  d. July 26, 1934, Little Rock, Ark.
  U. S. Senator, 1916-21
LEWIS, Meriwether
  b. Aug. 18, 1774, Albemarle County, Va.
  d. Oct. 11, 1809, in Tennessee
  Territorial governor (Louisiana District), 1806-09
LITTLE, John S.
  b. Mar. 15, 1853, Sebastian County, Ark.
  d. Oct. 29, 1916, Little Rock, Ark.
  U. S. Representative, 1894-1907
  Governor, 1907-09
McCULLOCH, Philip D., Jr.
  b. June 23, 1851, Murfreesboro, Tenn.
  d. Nov. 26, 1928, Marianna, Ark.
  U. S. Representative, 1893-1903
McDONALD, Alexander
  b. Apr. 10, 1832, Clinton County, Pa.
  d. Dec. 13, 1903, St. Lawrence County, N. Y.
  U. S. Senator, 1868-71
MACON, Robert B.
  b. July 6, 1859, Phillips County, Ark.
  d. Oct. 9, 1925, Marvell, Ark.
  U. S. Representative, 1903-13
McRAE, Thomas C.
  b. Dec. 21, 1851, Mt. Holly, Ark.
  d. June 2, 1929, Prescott, Ark.
  U. S. Representative, 1885-1903
  Governor, 1921-25
MARTINEAU, John E.
  b. Dec. 2, 1873, Clay County, Mo.
  d. Mar. 6, 1937, Little Rock, Ark.
  Governor, 1927-28

MILLER, James I.
  b. Apr. 25, 1776, Peterboro, N. H.
  d. July 7, 1851, Peterboro, N. H.
  Territorial governor, 1819-25
MILLER, William R.
  b. Nov. 27, 1823, Independence County, Ark.
  d. Nov. 27, 1887, Little Rock, Ark.
  Governor, 1877-81
MURPHY, Isaac
  b. Oct. 16, 1802, Pittsburgh, Pa.
  d. Sept. 8, 1882, Huntsville, Ark.
  Governor, 1864-68
NEILL, Robert
  b. Nov. 12, 1838, Independence County, Ark.
  d. Feb. 16, 1907, Independence County, Ark.
  U. S. Representative, 1893-97
NEWTON, Thomas W.
  b. Jan. 18, 1804, Alexandria, Va.
  d. Sept. 22, 1853, New York, N. Y.
  U. S. Representative, 1847
NORRELL, William F.
  b. Aug. 29, 1896, Ashley County, Ark.
  d. Feb. 15, 1961, Washington, D. C.
  U. S. Representative, 1939-61
OLDFIELD, William A.
  b. Feb. 4, 1874, Franklin, Ark.
  d. Nov. 19, 1928, Washington, D. C.
  U. S. Representative, 1909-28
PARKS, Tillman B.
  b. May 14, 1872, Lafayette County, Ark.
  d. Feb. 12, 1950, Washington, D. C.
  U. S. Representative, 1921-37
PARNELL, Harvey
  b. Feb. 28, 1880, Cleveland County, Ark.
  d. Jan. 16, 1936, Dermott, Ark.
  Governor, 1928-33

PEEL, Samuel W.
  b. Sept. 13, 1831, Independence County, Ark.
  d. Dec. 18, 1924, Bentonville, Ark.
  U. S. Representative, 1883-93
POPE, John
  b. 1770, Westmoreland, Va.
  d. July 12, 1845, Springfield, Ky.
  Territorial governor, 1829-35
  U. S. Senator (Ky.), 1807-13, 1837-43
RAGON, Heartsill
  b. Mar. 20, 1885, Dublin, Ark.
  d. Sept. 15, 1940, Ft. Smith, Ark.
  U. S. Representative, 1923-33
RECTOR, Henry M.
  b. May 1, 1816, Louisville, Ky.
  d. Aug. 12, 1899, Little Rock, Ark.
  Governor, 1860-62
REED, James B.
  b. Jan. 2, 1881, Lonoke County, Ark.
  d. Apr. 27, 1935, Little Rock, Ark.
  U. S. Representative, 1923-29
REID, Charles C.
  b. June 15, 1868, Clarksville, Ark.
  d. May 20, 1922, Little Rock, Ark.
  U. S. Representative, 1901-11
RICE, Benjamin F.
  b. May 26, 1828, East Otto, N. Y.
  d. Jan. 19, 1905, Tulsa, Okla.
  U. S. Senator, 1868-73
ROANE, John S.
  b. Jan. 8, 1817, Wilson County, Tenn.
  d. Apr. 8, 1867, Little Rock, Ark.
  Governor, 1849-52
ROBINSON, Joseph T.
  b. Aug. 26, 1872, Lonoke County, Ark.
  d. July 14, 1937, Washington, D. C.
  U. S. Representative, 1903-13
  Governor, 1913
  U. S. Senator, 1913-37

ROGERS, Anthony A. C.
  b. Feb. 14, 1821, Clarksville, Tenn.
  d. July 27, 1899, Los Angeles, Calif.
  U. S. Representative, 1869-71
ROGERS, John H.
  b. Oct. 9, 1845, Bertie County, N. C.
  d. Apr. 16, 1911, Little Rock, Ark.
  U. S. Representative, 1883-91
ROOTS, Logan H.
  b. Mar. 26, 1841, Perry County, Ill.
  d. May 30, 1893, Little Rock, Ark.
  U. S. Representative, 1868-71
RUST, Albert
  b. ca. 1800 in Virginia
  d. Apr. 3, 1870, El Dorado, Ark.
  U. S. Representative, 1855-57, 1859-61
SAWYER, Lewis E.
  b. June 24, 1867, Shelby County, Ark.
  d. May 5, 1923, Hot Springs, Ark.
  U. S. Representative, 1923
SEBASTIAN, William K.
  b. 1812, Hickman County, Tenn.
  d. May 20, 1865, Memphis, Tenn.
  U. S. Senator, 1848-61
SEVIER, Ambrose H.
  b. Nov. 10, 1801, Greene County, Tenn.
  d. Dec. 31, 1848, Little Rock, Ark.
  Territorial delegate, 1828-37
  U. S. Senator, 1837-48
SLEMONS, William F.
  b. Mar. 15, 1830, Weakley County, Tenn.
  d. Dec. 10, 1918, Monticello, Ark.
  U. S. Representative, 1873-81
SNYDER, Oliver P.
  b. Nov. 13, 1833, in Missouri
  d. Nov. 22, 1882, Pine Bluff, Ark.
  U. S. Representative, 1871-75

TAYLOR, Chester W.
  b. July 16, 1883, Verona, Miss.
  d. July 17, 1931, Pine Bluff, Ark.
  U. S. Representative, 1922-23
TAYLOR, Samuel M.
  b. May 25, 1852, Itawamba County, Miss.
  d. Sept. 13, 1921, Washington, D. C.
  U. S. Representative, 1913-21
TERRAL, Tom J.
  b. Dec. 21, 1884, Union Parish, La.
  d. Mar. 9, 1946, Little Rock, Ark.
  Governor, 1925-27
TERRY, David D.
  b. Jan. 31, 1881, Little Rock, Ark.
  d. Oct. 6, 1963, Little Rock, Ark.
  U. S. Representative, 1933-43
TERRY, William L.
  b. Sept. 27, 1850, Anson County, N. C.
  d. Nov. 4, 1917, Little Rock, Ark.
  U. S. Representative, 1891-1901
TILLMAN, John N.
  b. Dec. 13, 1859, Greene County, Mo.
  d. Mar. 9, 1929, Fayetteville, Ark.
  U. S. Representative, 1915-29
WALKER, James D.
  b. Dec. 13, 1830, Logan County, Ky.
  d. Oct. 17, 1906, Fayetteville, Ark.
  U. S. Senator, 1879-85
WALLACE, Robert M.
  b. Aug. 6, 1856, New London, Ark.
  d. Nov. 9, 1942, Magnolia, Ark.
  U. S. Representative, 1903-11
WARREN, Edmund A.
  b. May 2, 1818, Greene County, Ala.
  d. July 2, 1875, Prescott, Ark.
  U. S. Representative, 1853-55, 1857-59

WILKINSON, James
  b. 1757, Alvert County, Md.
  d. Dec. 28, 1825, Mexico City, Mex.
  Territorial governor (Louisiana District), 1805-06
WILSHIRE, William
  b. Sept. 8, 1830, Shwaneetown, Ill.
  d. Aug. 19, 1888, Washington, D. C.
  U. S. Representative, 1875-77
WINGO, Otis
  b. June 18, 1877, Weakley County, Tenn.
  d. Oct. 21, 1930, Baltimore, Md.
  U. S. Representative, 1913-30
YELL, Archibald
  b. 1797, in North Carolina
  d. Feb. 22, 1847, Burena Vista, Mexico
  U. S. Representative, 1837-39, 1845-46
  Governor, 1840-44

OUTLINE OF CONSTITUTION

OUTLINE OF CONSTITUTION

I. Boundaries

II. Declaration of Rights

Sec. 1. Source of power
Sec. 2. Freedom and independence
Sec. 3. Equality before the law
Sec. 4. Right of assembly and of petition
Sec. 5. Right to bear arms
Sec. 6. Liberty of the press and of speech; libel
Sec. 7. Jury trial; right to; waiver
Sec. 8. Criminal charges; self-incrimination; due process; double jeopardy; bail
Sec. 9. Excessive bail or punishment prohibited; witnesses; detention
Sec. 10. Rights of accused enumerated; change of venue
Sec. 11. Habeas corpus
Sec. 12. Suspension of laws
Sec. 13. Redress of wrongs
Sec. 14. Treason
Sec. 15. Unreasonable searches and seizures
Sec. 16. Imprisonment for debt
Sec. 17. Attainder; ex post facto laws
Sec. 18. Privileges and immunities; equality
Sec. 19. Perpetuities and monopolies
Sec. 20. Resident aliens; descent of property
Sec. 21. Life, liberty and property; banishment prohibited
Sec. 22. Property rights; taking without just compensation prohibited
Sec. 23. Eminent domain and taxation
Sec. 24. Religious liberty
Sec. 25. Protection of religion
Sec. 26. Religious tests
Sec. 27. Slavery; standing armies; military subordinate to civil power

VII. Judicial

VIII. Apportionment

Amendments

58   ARKANSAS

SELECTED DOCUMENTS

SELECTED DOCUMENTS

Among the early explorers of the trans-Mississippi area, Thomas Nuttall, an observant and widely-traveled naturalist, wrote extensively of his experiences on a series of trips within a decade of the Louisiana Purchase. His *Journal of Travels in the Arkansa Territory in the Year 1819* was published in 1821, and the excerpt reprinted here is a vignette of the area just as American settlements were beginning to push into it.

A post-bellum view of the Old South as it persisted in Arkansas is given in two articles by Octave Thanet in the *Atlantic Monthly* magazine for July and September 1891, on plantation life and town life in the state in the generation after the Civil War.

The most famous Arkansas contribution to American legend, however, is the song and related anecdotes of "The Arkansas Traveler," which like most folk tales has endless variations and an endless list of individuals and places which are supposed to be the source of the originals. G.W. Mercer, in the *Century* magazine for March 1896, was one of many who tried to run down some of the associations, and his article, "On the Track of the Arkansas Traveler," may be taken as typical of similar efforts before and since.

DOCUMENTS

TRAVELS IN THE ARKANSA TERRITORY
by Thomas Nuttall

To-day I was detained at Mr. M'Lane's, waiting the
drunken whim of the Yankee, whom necessity had obliged
me to hire. In the course of a few hours he had shift-
ed from two bargains. At first, I was to give him
five dollars for his assistance, and in case that
should prove inadequate, I had agreed to hire an addi-
tional hand on the Arkansa. Now he wished to have the
boat for bringing her completely to the Port, and next
he wanted 10 dollars!

I endeavoured to amuse myself in the neighborhood,
by a ramble through the adjoining cane-brake. Here I
found abundance of the *Celtis integrifolia* (entire-
leaved nettle tree) and the common and one-seeded
honey-locust; also *Forrestiera acuminata* of Poiret
(*Borya acuminata,* WILD.). The day was as mild and
warm as the month of May, and the *Senecio laciniata,*
so common along the banks of the Mississippi, already
showed signs of flowering.

To-day we proceeded up White river with considerable difficulty, and hard labour, the Mississippi not
being sufficiently high to produce any eddy. The
course which we made, in the two miles that we ascend-
ed, was west by north. I now found the boatman whom
I had hired, one of the most worthless and drunken
scoundrels imaginable; he could not be prevailed upon
to do any thing but steer, while myself and the other
man I had hired, were obliged to keep constantly to
the oar, or the cordelle (tow-rope). In the evening
we left the boat without any guard, intending to re-
pair to it in the morning from Mr. M'Lane's, where we
returned again this evening, being only three miles

distant across the forest. Here I discovered that the Yankee intended to proceed to the boat in our absence and rob me, pretending some business to the mouth of the Arkansa, for which he must depart by moon-light. Unknown to him, however, and accompanied by a young man whom I had hired in his place, we repaired the boat, waiting under arms the approach of the thief, but unable to obtain a boat, he had relinquished the attempt, and saved himself from chastisement.

In the neighbouring woods I was shewn a scandent leguminous shrub, so extremely tenacious as to afford a good substitute for ropes, and commonly employed as a boat's cable. A knot can be tied of it with ease. On examination I found it to be the plant which I have called *Wisteria speciosa (Glycine frutescens*. WILD.*)* the Carolina kidney-bean tree.

We continued with hard labour ascending White river to the bayou, said to enter seven miles up that stream. The latter proceeds from the bayou, in a direction of west to north-west, the bayou or cut-off continuing to the south-west. In this distance, there are no settle-ments, the land being overflowed by the back water of the Mississippi. We passed nearly through the bayou, in which there are four points of land and a half; the current carrying us almost three miles an hour towards the Arkansa, which it entered nearly at right angles, with a rapid current, and a channel filled with snags. The length of the bayou appears to be about eight or nine miles.

Leaving the bayou, we entered the Arkansa, which was very low, but still red and muddy from the fresh-ets of the Canadian. Most of the larger streams which enter into it from the south, are charged with red and turbid water, while those of the north are clear. Every where I observed the chocolate or reddish brown clay of the salt formation, deposited by the southern freshets. The Arkansa had here a very gentle current, and was scarcely more than 200 yards wide, with its

meanders on a small scale, similar to those of the
Mississippi. In consequence of the unrestrained
dominion of the inundation, no settlements yet appeared in this quarter. We proceeded chiefly by means of
the cordelle, but at a very tedious and tiresome rate,
for, after the utmost exertion, with our unwieldly
boat, we were this evening only six and a half miles
above the outlet of the bayou.

We found the labour of towing our boat exceedingly
tiresome, in consequence of the sudden falling of the
river, produced by a corresponding ebb of the Mississippi. With painful exertions, and after wading more
than three hours in the river, we passed only two
bars in the course of the day.

To-day we towed along two bars, much more considerable than any preceding bends, but had the disappoint-
ment to spend the night only a single mile below
Madame Gordon's, the place of our destination with the
boat, and only 16 miles above the bayou, by which we
entered the Arkansa. This house is the first which is
met with in ascending the river. Nearly opposite to
the foot of the last bar but one which we passed, a
vast pile of drift wood marks the outlet of a bayou,
which is open in high water, and communicates with the
Mississippi.

The three last bends of the river, like the four
first, tending by half circles to the north-west, are
each about two and three miles in circuit. As in the
Mississippi, the current sets with the greatest force
against the centre of the curves; the banks of which
are nearly perpendicular, and subject to a perpetual
state of dislocation. In such situations we frequently
see brakes of cane; while, on the opposite side, a
naked beach of sand, thinly strewed with succulent
and maritime plants, considerably wider than the river,
appears to imitate the aridity of a desert, though
contrasted at a little distance by skirting groves of
willows and poplars.

No other kind of soil appears than a friable loam,
and the beds of red clay, which so strongly tinge the
water at particular periods of inundation. The sand
of the river appears to be in perpetual motion, drifting along at the beck of the current; its instability
is indeed often dangerous to the cattle that happen to
venture into the river, either to drink or traverse
the stream.

The land, although neglected, appears in several
places, below Madame Gordon's, high enough to be sus-
ceptible of cultivation, and secure from inundation,
at least for some distance from the immediate bank of
the river.

No change, that I can remark yet exists in the veg-
etation, and the scenery is almost destitute of every
thing which is agreeable to human nature; nothing yet
appears but one vast trackless wilderness of trees, a
dead solemnity, where the human voice is never heard
to echo, where not even ruins of the humblest kind
recal its history to mind, or prove the past dominion
of man. All is rude nature as it sprang into existence,
still preserving its primeval type, its unreclaimed ex-
uberance.

This morning we had extremely hard labour, to tow
the only mile which remained of our tiresome voyage.
I was obliged to plunge into the water up to the waist,
and there work for some time, to disengage the boat
from a hidden log upon which it was held; the men I had
employed, being this morning scarcely willing to wet
their feet, although I had to pay them exorbitant wages.

A mile and a half from Madame Gordon's, there was a
settlement, consisting of four or five French families,
situated upon an elevated tract of fertile land, which
is occasionally insulated by the overflowings of the
White and Arkansa rivers.

To-day, and indeed for more than a week past, the
weather, except being cloudy, has felt to me like May;
towards mid-day, the thermometer rose to 67°. The

birds had commenced their melodies; and on the high and
open bank of the river near to Madame Gordon's, I had
already the gratification of finding flowers of the
same natural family as many of the early plants of Europe; the Cruciferae; but to me they were doubly interesting, as the first fruits of a harvest never before
reaped by any botanist.

In the afternoon, I walked about a mile from the river to the house of Monsieur Tenass, an honest and indus-
trious farmer. The crop of cotton, and of corn, here
the last summer was, I understand, very indifferent,
for want of rain. The first sold here, at five to six
dollars per hundred weight, in the seed; and flour at
10 dollars per barrel.

The climate is said to be too warm for apples, but
quite suitable for peaches. The land on which this
gentleman and his neighbours resided, in tolerable independence, is very considerably elevated and open,
bearing a resemblance to the lands about the Chicasaw
Bluffs, and at first view, I thought I discovered a
considerable hill, but it was, in fact, an enormous
mound, not less than 40 feet high, situated towards the
centre of a circle of other lesser mounds, and elevated
platforms of earth. The usual vestiges of earthenware,
and weapons of hornstone flint, are here also met with,
scattered over the surrounding soil.

In any other direction from this settlement, the
lands are totally overflowed in freshets as far as the
Mississippi. On this side of the Arkansa, the floods
cover the whole intermediate space to White river, a
distance of 30 miles. Within this tract, cultivation
can never take place without recourse to the same industry, which has redeemed Holland from the ocean. The
singular caprice of the river, as it accidentally seeks
its way to the sea, meandering through its alluvial
valley, is truly remarkable. The variation of its channel is almost incredible, and the action which it exer-
cises over the destiny of the soil, can scarcely be

conceived. After pursuing a given course for many ages, and slowly encroaching, it has, at length, in many instances cut through an isthmus, and thus abandoned perhaps a course of six or eight miles, in which the water stagnating, at length becomes totally insulated, and thus presents a lagoon or lake. One of these insulated channels, termed a lake, commences about two miles from hence, and approaches within four miles of the Arkansas or the Post of Osark, affording a much nearer communication than the present course of the river.

Towards evening, two keel boats came in sight, one of which was deeply loaded with whiskey and flour; the other, a small boat fitted out by a general Calamees and his brother, two elderly men out on a land speculation, who intended to ascend the river as far as the Cadron, which is 300 miles from hence by water, or to the Fort, which is 350 miles further. I perceived that they noted down every particular which came to their knowledge, but appeared to be illiterate men, and of course, I found them incapable of appreciating the value of science. On application, they merely condescended to offer me a passage, provided I would find my own provision, and work as a boat-man. Such was the encouragement, which I at length wrung from these generous speculators; not, I dare say, exploring the Missouri territory with the same philanthropic views as the generous Birkbeck.

About 12 o'clock, the thermometer was again at 67°. In the course of the forenoon, I took a solitary ramble down the bank of the river, and found along its shelving border, where the sun obtained free access, abundance of the *Mimosa glandulosa* of Michaux; also *Polypremum procumbens, Diodia virginica, Verbena nodiflora,* Lin. *Eclipta erecta,* Mich. *Poa stricta, Panicum capillaceum, Poa reptans* as usual in vast profusion, and *Capraria multifida.* The trees and shrubs are chiefly the Pecan, *(Carya olivoeformis) C. aquatica;* the black walnut,

(*Juglans nigra*), but very rare; *Fraxinus quadrangulata,
Liquidamber* and *Platanus*, but rarely large or full grown;
also *Celtis integrifolia;* the swamp oak *(Quercus aquatica)*, nearly sempervirent, the red oak *(Q. rubra)*, the
scarlet oak *(Q. coccinea)*, Spanish oak *(Q. falcata)*;
Populus angulisans, the cotton wood, of greater magnitude than any other tree in this country, with the wood
yellowish, like that of the Tulip tree, answering the
purpose of fence rails, and being tolerably durable.
The smaller white poplar *(P. monilifera)*, never so large
as the preceding, commonly growing in groves like the
willows, and presenting a bark which is white and even.
Different kinds of honey locust, as the common species
Gleditscia triacanthos, the one-seeded *G. monosperma*,
and the short podded *G. brachyloba*. There is no sugar-
maple, as I understand, nearer than the upper parts of
the St. Francis and White river.

The alluvial soil is here sandy and light; by no
means luxuriant, except on the very margin of the river.
We no where see such enormous trees as those which so
frequently occur along the banks of the Ohio; this, however, may in part be occasioned by the instability of
the soil, from whence they are occasionally swept at no
very distant intervals. The tulip tree *(Lyriodendron
tulipifera)*, which attains the acme of its perfection
and magnitude in Kentucky, is not met with on the banks
of the Arkansa.

In consequence of the many saline streams which fall
into this river, its waters are frequently found to be
almost impotable.

The path, which I this morning pursued to the Post,
now town of Arkansas, passed through remarkably contrasted situations and soil. After leaving the small
circumscribed and elevated portion of settled lands already noticed, and over which were scattered a number
of aboriginal mounds, I entered upon an oak swamp,
which, by the marks on the trees, appeared to be usually
inundated, in the course of the summer, four to six feet

by the back water of the river. The species are prin-
cipally *Quercus lyrata, Q. macrocarpa* (the over-cup
oak); *Q. Phellos* (the willow oak); *Q. falcata* (the
Spanish oak); and *Q. palustris* (the swamp oak); with
some red and scarlet, as well as black and post oak on
the knolls, or more elevated parts. In this swamp, I
also observed the *Nyssa aquatica, N. pubescens* (Ogechee
lime, the fruit being prepared as a conserve), as well
as *N. biflora,* and *Gleditscia monosperma*. After crossing this horrid morass, a delightful tract of high
ground again occurs, over which the floods had never
yet prevailed; here the fields of the French settlers
were already of a vivid green, and the birds were singing from every bush, more particularly the red bird
(Loxia cardinalis), and the blue sparrow *(Motacilla
sialis)*. The ground appeared perfectly whitened with
the *Alyssum bidentatum*. The *Viola bicolor,* the *Myosu-
rus minimus* of Europe, (probably introduced by the
French settlers) and the *Houstonia serpyllifolia* of
Michaux, *(H. patens* of Mr. Elliott) with bright blue
flowers, were also already in bloom. After emerging
out of the swamp, in which I found it necessary to
wade about ankle deep, a prairie came in view, with
scattering houses spreading over a narrow and elevated
tract for about three miles parallel to the bend of the
river.

On arriving, I waited on Monsieur Bougie, one of
the earliest settlers and principal inhabitants of the
place, to whom I was introduced by letter. I soon
found in him a gentleman, though disguised at this time
in the garb of a Canadian boatman. He treated me with
great politeness and respect, and, from the first in-
terview, appeared to take a generous and active interest in my favour. Monsieur B. was by birth a Canadian,
and, though 70 years of age, possessed almost the vig-
our and agility of youth. This settlement owes much
to his enterprise and industry.

The town, or rather settlement of the Post of Arkan-

sas, was somewhat dispersed over a prairie, nearly as
elevated as that of the Chicasaw Bluffs, and contain-
ing in all between 30 and 40 houses. The merchants,
then transacting nearly all the business of the Arkansa and White river, were Messrs. Braham and Drope, Mr.
Lewis, and Monsieur Notrebe, who kept well-assorted
stores of merchandize, supplied chiefly from New Orleans, with the exception of some heavy articles of
domestic manufacture obtained from Pittsburgh. Mr.
Drope, to whom I was also introduced by letter, received me with politeness, and I could not but now for
awhile consider myself as once more introduced into the
circle of civilization.

The improvement and settlement of this place proceeded slowly, owing, in some measure, as I am informed,
to the uncertain titles of the neighbouring lands.
Several enormous Spanish grants remained still undecid-
ed; that of Messrs. Winters, of Natchez, called for no
less than one million of acres, but the congress of the
United States, inclined to put in force a kind of agra-
rian law against such monopolizers, had laid them, as I
was told, under the stipulation of settling upon this
immense tract a certain number of families.

The cotton produced in this neighbourhood, of a
quality no way inferior to that of Red river, obtained
this year from six to six and a half dollars per cwt.
in the seed, and there were now two gins established
for its preparation, though, like every thing else, in
this infant settlement of the poor and improvident, but
little attention beyond that of absolute necessity, was
as yet paid to any branch of agriculture. Nature has
here done so much, and man so little, that we are yet
totally unable to appreciate the value and resources of
the soil. Amongst other kinds of grain, rice has been
tried on a small scale, and found to answer every ex-
pectation. The price of this grain, brought from New
Orleans, was no less than 25 to 37½ cents per lb. by
retail. Under the influence of a climate mild as the

south of Europe, and a soil equal to that of Kentucky, wealth will ere long flow, no doubt, to the banks of the Arkansa.

I again made application to the land speculators, trying to prevail upon them on any terms, to take up my baggage, as far as the Cadron, which would have enabled me immediately to proceed on my journey, across the great prairie, but they remained inexorable.

To-day, I returned to Madame Gordon's, which, though only six miles distant by land, is not less than 15 by water. I was now obliged more deeply to wade through the enswamped forests, which surround the habitable prairie lands, in consequence of the late rain. In these ponds, I am told, the Proteus or Syren is occasionally met with. There are also alligators, though by no means numerous.

This morning I again proceeded up the river with my flat boat, by the assistance of two French boatmen, full of talk, and, at first, but indifferently inclined to work; we succeeded, however, by night, to get to the third of the five sand-bars or bends, which intervene between this place and the village of Arkansas. The following day in the evening, after a good deal of hard labour and wading, on my part, and that of the negro in my employ, we arrived at Monsieur Bougie's, and the next day I parted with a sort of regret from the boat, which, with all its difficulties, had afforded me, through the most inclement season of the year, no inconsiderable degree of comfort and convenience.

On the 26th, I proceeded with my baggage and property to the village in Monsieur Bougie's perogue, accompanied by one boatman. Near to the town, we grounded on the inner side of a recent, and still augmenting bar and, after falling a little back, we crossed over, but here the current would not permit us to advance with the oars. The shore was high, and the water too deep for poles, so that we had again to attempt the side we had left; here, in drifting with velocity again on the

and space and beauty. He has, too, a rude plenty for
his material wants. And is it not to be counted that
one shall have the key to the fields; the right to
live close to the grass, to miss the cankerfret of
envy, the suffocation of merciless crowds, the sick
despair of failure, and the untiring goad of fear?

Yes, we may weave our complacent plans to "elevate"
this people; but I question, Do they need our pity?
They are what Montaigne dubbed himself, "unpremedi-
tated and accidental philosophers."

Neither need our kind friends of civilization pity
our plight on "that forlorn plantation." We are
amazingly comfortable, thank you. For one thing, -
but there are many things! - to win the best out of
life, one must live at least part of the time in the
country, I mean the real country; not the country of
Watteau and fetes, where nature is but a splendid
canvas on which to paint fine toilets and field
sports.

A plantation has all the simple charm of a farm
without its loneliness. Here there is always a small
ripple of human interest to watch, - like that picture from my window at this moment, for instance: a
stalwart black fellow breaking a colt. To wake in
the morning to the country sounds, a cock crowing
lustily, a mocking-bird singing, the ring of an axe,
the whistle of the little black boy driving the cows
to pasture, the swash of the river waves, the soft
stir of the wind in the cypress brake; at night, to
watch the sunset burn out in the west, or the horse-
men riding home with their bags of meal flung over
their saddle-bow, or the herds winding along the
woodland road, listening, at the same time, to the
lowing of the cows and the bleat of the lambs, and
now and again to a distant yodel or the boat song
of Peps steering up a raft of logs, - here are simple
pleasures, but they leave no sting.

Another thing that we enjoy is that we may be

friends with the poor.

Perhaps it will be said that we may - and should - be friends with the poor everywhere. I will wager a basket of Arkansas roses against a handful of chips that the objector has not a single friend among the real poor. Do you call that woman with the six small children, who comes each morning for your skimmed milk, your friend; or the beneficiaries of your different most worthy societies, whom you barely know apart? If you do, you deceive yourself, and the truth is not in you. Your friend is himself, by his own name and person, interesting to you; the skimmed-milk woman is only a poor creature to you, that you help because you are benevolent, and from whom you expect vast gratitude or little, according to your temperament. O you unconscious inspirer of anarchists!

But to know the poor as individuals, not as "the poor," to be made free of their sorrows, to see their piteous little pleasures, to be friends, - that is different, that is to feel the eternal kinship. Bring your gift to a poor renter's wedding, or go for a few minutes to his merry-making, - spring, when windows and doors are open, is the preferable time; talk with him over your woodpile that he comes to chop, until you know all about the oldest girl, who "kin jest take up a book and read right spang off, - don't have to stop to spell nary," - and the baby, "the smartest little trick you ever did see;" sit all night in the draughts of his cabin watching a dying child (nothing like such an experience to fetch the necessity for comfortable houses for your tenants home to your conscience!); and when the importunity of death to spare has failed, learn how alike are all mothers' hearts in their desolation, - and you will comprehend the difference. Such an intercourse brings a feeling that is nearer and more human than could come of years of perfunctory interest as a "kind lady."

To these people we are only their good neighbors;
more generous - not more kind - than other neighbors,
simply because we have more to give. They are at-
tached to us as "mighty nice, pleasant, 'bliging folks."
They feel no wound to their pride in accepting favors
that they would return were it in their power; indeed,
do return in other shapes. Surely, in this day and
generation, when Samson strains at the pillars of the
temple, it is a thing worth counting, this wholesome
and gentle relation.

For myself, I count it a further mercy that we live
among a people so honest, kindly, and unhasty. It is
a rest to be out of the nineteenth century for a while,
with people who will not hurry for money, who believe
in Jonah and the whale (all the more stanchly that
they have but the dimmest notion what a whale is),
and consider theft worse than murder.

Soon it will all be changed. Already the shadow
creeps over the dial.

Just as the ugly, comfortable new houses are
replacing the picturesque old cabins, as the "heater"
stove is crowding out the fireplace, so the new ways
will push the old aside. The school-children do not
talk dialect; only the old people are willing to plant
corn by hand.

Some day a railway station will be the magnet for
the loungers instead of the store, or -- oh, heavy
thought! - there will be no more loungers. We shall
all be civilized into stirring Philistines, with no
time to waste in friendly gossip; farms will be
tilled by tenants who expect to make money as well as
a livelihood, and could not shoot a wild turkey to
save their lives; the saw will buzz away our grand
old forests that have sheltered the mound-builders;
we shall become a syndicate, or a corporation, or a
trust; and the country will be so well drained that
it cannot even summon an old-time chill over its
changed conditions.

Yes, the new civilization will come. I am enough
a child of my age to feel that it is best it should
come, but I am glad to be here before it comes. I
hope that it may not come too fast!

> "Touch us gently, Time!
> We've not proud nor soaring wings;
> Our ambition, our content,
> Lies in simple things.
> Humble voyagers are we
> O'er Life's dim, unbounded sea,
> Seeking only some calm clime; -
> Touch us gently, gentle Time!"

TOWN LIFE IN ARKANSAS.

Octave Thanet.

To an inhabitant of a great city a chapter on town life in Arkansas may seem likely to be almost as concise as the famous one on snakes in Ireland. There is no great city in Arkansas, and only four towns can claim more than ten thousand inhabitants, - Little Rock, Fort Smith, Pine Bluff, and Hot Springs. The largest of these has less than fifty thousand. Nevertheless there is a distinct difference between the life of the town dweller in Arkansas and that of a man in the rural districts. For that matter, there are minor differences among the citizens of towns strongly enough marked to impress a stranger.

The semi-Northern bustle and vigor of Fort Smith, the repose and hospitality of Little Rock, the African din and humor and the tropical aspect of Pine Bluff, have as little likeness one to another as any of them can have to the unique chaos that we know as Hot Springs. The visitor might imagine the breadth of States between them, only always Southern States. In my fancy, often I relegate them to their proper kindred. Fort Smith is a Georgian town; Little Rock belongs about equally to South Carolina and Virginia; Pine Bluff might have been taken bodily out of Mississippi; Hot Springs - but I have already said Hot Springs can be compared to no town but itself.

Between the denizens of small towns and large, as we reckon size in Arkansas, there is an appreciable line of social demarcation. To speak frankly, the large-town man has in a great measure come into the current of modern civilization. Even when he does not belong to the more educated class, he is a vastly more civilized being than his brother of the same rank in the country or the village. He is more alert,

more impressionable, he talks better English, he reads
the newspaper, he would like th Arkansas legislature
to vote a generous appropriation for the World's Fair.
In short, he is of the New South.

Every traveler going south from St. Louis can re-
call the average Arkansas village in winter. Little
strings of houses spread raggedly on both sides of
the rails. A few wee shops, that are likely to have
a mock rectangle of facade stuck against a triangle
of roof, in the manner of children's card houses,
parade a draggled stock of haberdashery and groceries.
To right or left a mill buzzes, its newness attested
by the raw tints of the weather boarding. There is
no horizon; there seldom is a horizon in Arkansas, -
it is cut off by the forest. Pools of water reflect
the straight black lines of tree trunks and the crook-
ed lines of bare boughs, while a muddy road winds
through the vista. Generally there are a few lean
cattle to stare in a dejected fashion at the train,
and some fat black swine to root among the sodden
grasses. Bales of cotton are piled on the railway
platform, and serve as seats for half a dozen list-
less men in high boots and soft hats. Occasionally,
a woman, who has not had the time to brush her hair,
calls shrilly to some child who is trying to have
pneumonia by sitting on the ground. No one seems to
have anything to do, yet every one looks tired, and
the passenger in the Pullman wonders how people live
in "such a hole."

Two months later the "hole" will have changed into
a garden. The great live oaks will wave a glossy
foliage of richest green. Men will be ploughing in
the fields, and the negroes' song will float through
the open car window. The house yards will be abloom
with Japan quince and lilacs. The very shop windows
will have a dash of fresh color in summer bonnets
and piles of new prints. Then the stranger will
awake to the charm of the South; and were one to

He smiled his gentlest, timidest smile; a baby
could not look more guileless.

"Colored boy, he jumped on me t'other night, and I
cut him," simpered Don.

"With a razor, I suppose?"

"Yes'm."

"Did you kill him?"

"No, ma'am. Doctor reckons he'll be out soon."

The end of the matter was that I gave Don a little
money to pacify the feelings of the cut boy, which
was done so successfully that Don's amiable smile
was waiting in the same place to greet me when I
returned.

I would not mention this trifling incident were it
not that it illustrates the negro character. Don
felt the same embarrassment over his unsuccessful
homicide that one of another race might have felt
over a rather rough practical joke at which the vic-
tim was unreasonably angry; and at the same time he
had the black man's pathetic confidence in his "folks."

The same combination of absence of moral sense with
childlike trustfulness was shown by Albert, another
of our valuable boys. One day, in an "all sorts
store," he was bragging with a pistol, and was so
unlucky as to shoot off part of his thumb, and to be
arrested for carrying concealed weapons into the
bargain. When they had put him in jail, he spent
all his time at the window looking out for some of
us to come to town. "Mr. Planter or Miss----won't
let me stay here long, if I git sight on 'em," the
poor fellow said. We had to patch up some sort of
a compromise with justice out of sheer pity for his
faith in us, by virtue of which Albert worked his
fine out on the sheriff's farm very comfortably.

All this is not to deny that there is crime, or
deplorable failure of justice, or mob violence in
Arkansas; but the outrages are irregular, not the
customary thing. Really, the lawlessness is largely

an imported lawlessness, while the occasional failure of justice is due to the costliness of convic-
tions and the poverty of the State. This was noto-
riously the fact in the Clayton tragedy. The murder-
ers were known to the grand jury, a member of which
assured me that only the utter bareness of the state
treasury prevented their conviction; but they had
fled the State, and the State was not rich enough to
pursue them. A kind of fury of impatience at such a
condition of things is at the bottom of much of the
summary execution of punishment. Ignorant men, who
yet know very well the connection between their own
pockets and the taxes, reason: "Why should we spend
thirty thousand dollars to give the bloody scoundrel
every legal chance to escape his just deserts? Shoot
him down and save the money!"

It has been the unhappy fate of the State to be a
house of refuge for human failures of all kinds.
Desperadoes fleeing from justice or seeking their
prey, broken-down adventurers, bankrupts, poverty-
stricken movers who have fled before the sheriff, -
all have flocked up the river, down the river, across
the country- to poor Arkansas. Crime could hide in
her trackless forest, and even the "trifling" could
scratch a living out of her fertile fields. There
was a time when the "land of the bowie knife" did
not belie its name, but that time has passed, and in
no other part of the country, not in New England,
certainly not in the West, can I remember to have met
with such a simple reverence for the law as law as
one can find in most Arkansas villages. Of the
cities I do not speak now; they are under different
conditions.

A photograph of a village in Arkansas would not be
complete without a view of the village newspaper.
The Arkansas country newspaper is a weekly journal
full of the humanities. The rural newspaper is always a mirror. But these small Arkansas papers

return more truthfully the reflection of their local-
ity because they fill their columns with news from
different little villages adjacent that have no paper of their own. The letters are by local corres-
pondents, and are highly natural. The painstaking
editor, who is often the printer as well, amends the
spelling and corrects the grammar according to his
lights (lights sometimes rather dim), and washes his
hands of the rest. Thus, on the same page of the
paper before me, I find "Swampy's" prediction that
"no man can carry the United States for President
in 1893 who is not for free silver," and in the very
next column behold "D. K." hurrahing for "Cleveland
and his silver letter," and shouting, "Let the battle
cry be Cleveland, free trade, and honest money!"
Some of the expressions sound strangely to an Eastern
ear; for example, this from the editor's own muse:
"Circuit court was in session, and after a howdy with
the affable clerk," etc.

Here is a paragraph describing the drowning of a
boy: "The body was gotten out three or four hours
after, and was interred the same day, and has gone
to meet the father of long years of suffering, and
also some brothers who have gone before. Freddy was
a good boy." The same sheet, in an earlier issue,
used a striking but friendly frankness regarding the
"Widow C----," who had come to town with her cotton.
"The widow," says the kindly editor, "is the right
type of widow, and moves on with a firm but sure
step to the goal. Her son Tommy is a great help to
her. Tommy is a good boy and honors his mother, and
his days shall be long in the land."

Indeed, every page radiates an intimate friendli-
ness. Has Squire Leens broken his leg, the correspondent condoles, mentioning in warm terms how use-
fully and nimbly the squire would otherwise employ
that imprisoned limb. "Mrs. Rev. Jones," who has
"a severe attack of the La Grippe," and Miss Nettie

Howard, who "is suffering from a rising in her ear,"
each has a whole paragraph of sympathy. Numerous
jocose though mysterious allusions enable us, if not
the editor, to guess why young "Bud Harrington comes
over to our town so often these moonlight nights.
Nice, driving with one hand moonlight nights, is n't
it, Bud? As Shakespeare or some other poet author
says, 'There's nothing half so sweet in life as love's
young dream.' That's so!" In this fashion of pleas-
antry does the wit of the writers disport itself.
Frequently, like Mr. Wegg, they drop into poetry.
The rhyme is of a free and generous turn, despising
the clogging fetters of metre. I have a specimen
before me. A correspondent tells of the death of a
"prominent citizen," and expresses sympathy for his
widow, concluding: --

> "Oh, may Mrs. Hotchkiss' path be lit
> With consolation from on high;
> And may they all live in righteous ways
> Until they come to die."

Thus on, piously if not poetically, through three
stanzas. The editor blesses all the brides and
praises all the babies. Not in his columns shall you
find the ill-bred sneers of his Northern brother in
regard to mothers-in-law. He doffs his hat and bows.
Once, at the top of an editorial column, I read,
"Our mother-in-law, Mrs. S----, is in town."

The country paper has an atmosphere of good will,
whatever else you may find in it; not always delicate,
but never malicious. The same atmosphere pervades
the people's lives. In one of Miss Wilkins's admi-
rable miniatures she pictures two old maiden sisters
who genteelly starve together. One day a prying
neighbor comes into their dining-room. They are at
tea. Their dainty table belongings, their pitiful
fare, are exposed to "Matilda Jenkins's" devouring
eyes. "Nothing did they guard so sacredly as the
privacy of their meals." The younger sister is

overwhelmed, but the elder sister rises to the crisis.
"Come into the other room" she says, with stately
dignity, and sweeps the prying Matilda before her.
Such a scene would be impossible in an Arkansas town.
Had the sisters lived in an Arkansas town, and had
Matilda Jenkins, let her motive be evil as it might,
crossed their threshold at a meal-time, she must
inevitably have been bidden to "dror up," "rest her
hat on the bed," and "take a bite." But then, in an
Arkansas town Matilda Jenkins would not have pried.

To every one his due; we have the virtues of our
vices in Arkansas. We may be improvident, we may
(though I am not so sure of that) lack sustained
energy, we may be hot-headed and unjust, but we are
not inquisitive, we are not censorious; we are hospi-
table and kindly affectioned one to another. And
these qualities oil the jarring wheels of daily life.
They seem to harmonize with the climate. Perhaps one
main reason for our unbounded hospitality is, that in
an Arkansas village there is no strain to keep up
appearances. One cannot imagine two Arkansas sisters
with one gown in common, like Miss Wilkins's pathetic
spinsters, laboriously ripping off the lace and put-
ting on velvet to pass it off on the neighbors as
two. No; the Southerner would say, "Ain't it lucky
sister's dress fits me?" and with all the neighbors
discuss trimming it.

If one of the New Englanders so delicately painted
by Miss Wilkins were to have shoes too ragged to
mend, she would stay away from the sewing society
because she had "laid out to clean the house, and all
was done except one room, and she could n't feel comfortable till she got that done" (carefully leaving
the room undone to make her words good), or because
her head ached, or because of some other equally
respectable and valid reason. The Arkansan would --
in fact, the Arkansan did -- push out a small foot
in the wreck of a shoe, saying: "Why, yes, ma'am, I'd

like to come best in the world, and I could come, but
my shoes do look so distressed I'm ashamed. Reckon
you'll have to excuse me till I git a new pair."

Having nothing to conceal, a guest is made welcome
to his host's little as heartily as to his abundance.
On the guest's part, he -- or especially she -- ex-
pects to lend a friendly hand at the kitchen stove
or at the pump outside. Where in a New England or
New York or Pennsylvania town will one find whole
families going out to spend the day in homes out of
their circle of kindred? But in an Arkansas village
it is the commonest thing for "all the Joneses," including the favorite among the Jones dogs and at
least two of the Jones horses, to go to spend Sunday
with the Smiths; or all the Smiths, from old man
Smith to his visiting grandchild, to dine with the
Joneses.

Mr. Howells, referring to Miss Wilkins's tales,
makes a trenchant criticism. He says: "What our
artist has done is to catch the American look of life,
so that if her miniatures remain to other ages they
shall know just the expression of that vast average
of Americans who do the hard work of the country and
live narrowly on their small earnings and savings.
If there is no gayety in that look, it is because the
face of hard work is always sober, and because the
consciousness of merciless fortuities and inexorable
responsibilities comes early and stays late with our
people." Let Mr. Howells except in great measure
the Southern workers from his characterization. The
face of hard work in the South wears an amiable smile
that broadens to a grin where that face is carved in
ebony. May not here be the secret of the intangible
but potent charm of Southern life?

An Arkansas village cannot be compared, in regard
to neat outlines and fresh paint and general prosper-
ity, to a village in New England. But if we are
less comfortable, we are vastly more happy, somehow;

we have let the sunshine in on poverty! In the South
we are not ashamed of being poor; therefore we do not
work our brains and our hearts and our consciences to
a thread trying to cover up our meagre living. Any
one can see it; yes, and any one may share it. More-
over, being less ambitious, we have leisure to enjoy
small pleasures, to do small courtesies. Even the
"mean man" of an Arkansas village is forced by om-
nipotent public opinion to be kind. Nobody is too
busy to lean over the fence and exchange a good
story with a passing neighbor. In the shops, the
bargaining always puts on a jocose air of *camaraderie*.
"Say, Mr. Trader," says the customer, "cayn't you
split this here plaid woolen suit and give me jest
a coat and vest?" "No, Billy," answers the shop-
keeper, weighing out sugar at the other end of the
store. "I'd like to the best in the world; but them's
plumb new goods, and I could n't nohow. But we got
some mighty nice black alpaccy goods; heap more comfortable, this weather. You lift that box behind
you and you'll see 'em; take 'em out and look 'em
over. If you open the blind over there, you can see
better. Shake it a little fust and it'll come; it's
got a sort o' stick to it. Thank ye."
    Arkansans are social souls, especially Arkansas
with black skins. They can spend hours in an "all
sorts store" or on a tavern veranda, coversing and
expectorating with slow zest in the moment. The
bursts of laughter that roll out from such a group
do not come from black throats alone; the Arkansas
villager enjoys a joke, and has a good share of the
grim Western drollery colored by some more vivid and
richer grotesqueness that may be the product of the
fervid sun. Western humor has a cynical streak;
good-natured as it is, there is in it a toleration,
born not only of large opportunities and a liberal
nature, but of low expectations of men, -- in fine,
the toleration of contempt rather than of charity.

But Southwestern humor is broad, rich, and gentle.
It is the humor of men who have plenty to eat, not
wrested from other men, but taken out of the ground.
No doubt the Gallic element in the native Arkansan
has done its hare in burnishing his wit as well as
shaping his manners. So far, the effect of the
continually swelling stream of Northern immigration
has only been to increase his energy without effacing
his genial qualities.

But I neglect the large towns; yet why not, since
all the large towns, notably the most bizarre and
picturesque of all Arkansas towns, Hot Springs, have
already been described very completely? And ade-
quately to portray Little Rock, Fort Smith, or Pine
Bluff would require a far larger canvas than is mine
in this article. The most sharply defined figures
in these large towns are the unreconstructed aris-
tocrats, now for the most part of the feminine gender.
They are as stanch and as pathetic, poor souls, as
Scott's Jacobits, with their locks of hair, and
battered swords, and thin old silver, and hoard of
bitter or splendid memories. I can foresee some
future novelist paying them a half-humorous, half-
affectionate respect, when time shall have healed
all the scars of war. These mourners over the past
always use one plaint whenever anything is praised:
"Ah, you should have seen it before the war!" A
story is told of a Little Rock old gentlewoman, who
was so constantly bemoaning the contrast of the
shabby present with the past that once, when the
moonlight was admired by her guest, out of sheer
force of habit she sighed, "Yes, ma'am, but oh, you
should have seen our moonlight before the war!"

Gentlemen and gentlewomen are so much the same the
world over, however, that one feels grateful even
for the minor differences. In the North a gentleman
is forced to be a man of the world; but in the South
a gentleman may still remain a provincial. The

Southern man of the world is, as all who know him
will admit, a charming fellow. He has a manner of
the gentlest suavity. Indeed, there is an ornate
leisure to his politeness that one does not often
perceive in colder and busier climes. His speech is
more studied, more decorated, than his Northern brother's; at the same time it is less artificial than
the models of his youth. He is dainty in his toilets,
clinging to the black frock coat, and he likes to
put himself into full dress. He cares more for society than Northerners of his class, and he is not
so careful to conceal his enthusiasms. But he is the
most tolerant of men and the most receptive. If back
in his soul there are fiery instincts and deeply
rooted prejudices of social order and race, an habit-
ual courtesy holds the curtains close. Nevertheless,
charming though he be, my heart yearns toward the
provincial, whose language slips occasionally into
the vernacular, who wears muddy boots, and from whose
Southern prejudices and ideals the world has not
brushed the bloom. He is a planter out of the way
of railways, helping, pushing, kicking, his tenants
into better ways of living; he is a lawyer in a
country town; he is a rural banker or merchant; he
is a clergy man with a parish large enough to be a
diocese; he is a country doctor, the unknown yet
valued correspondent of a great medical journal,
serving his profession far more successfully than his
own fortune, on horseback half his days, and sitting
up half his nights to study: but under whatever form-
al title, he is the same honest gentleman. Rustic
and aristocrat in a breath, he has the prejudices
of both his orders; so, likewise, he has their virtues, being frank, simple, loyal, and the helper of
the helpless. Take him all in all, the Arkansan,
with his Italian climate, his wonderful soil and
forests and mines, his mixed ancestry, his background
of mediaeval savagery, and his real awakening to

modern forces, is a figure instinct with possibili-
ties.

Do not judge him by the imbecilities of his legislature or the brutal outbreaking of the State's worst
and smallest element: the legislator is the representative of the carelessness of the State, not of its
real feeling; and the violence affects but an insignif-
icant section. The sense of a country never makes
the noise, and there is vastly more sense among rural
Arkansans, even on the subject of money legislation,
than would appear.

Life in Arkansas is more attractive than any one
who does not live in the State will believe. It has
elements which all American life would be the better
for absorbing. Perhaps I am not making too strong a
statement if I say that the North may have quite as
much to learn of the South as the South has to learn
of the North; and those of us who love both sections
with all our hearts please ourselves by dreaming that
the light of the North and the sweetness of the South
may some day blend like the melody of a tune, -- with
infinite variations, let us say, but no discords.

ON THE TRACK OF "THE ARKANSAS TRAVELER."

H. C. Mercer

SOMETIME about the year 1850 the American musical
myth known as "The Arkansas Traveler" came into vogue
among fiddlers. It is a quick reel tune, with a backwoods story talked to it while played, that caught the
ear at "side shows" and circuses, and sounded over the
trodden turf of fair grounds. Bands and foreign-bred
musicians were above noticing it, but the people loved
it and kept time to it, while tramps and sailors car-
ried it across seas to vie merrily in Irish cabins
with "The Wind that Shakes the Barley" and "The Soldier's Joy." With or without the dialogue, the music
was good for the humor, and it would have shown to the
musical antiquary, if he had noticed it, the boundary
line between the notes of nature and the notes of art
as clearly as "Strasburg" or "Prince Eugene" or "The
Boyne Water" or "Dixie."
    It lost nothing where showmen caught it from West-
ern adventurers in the days before the Union Pacific
Railroad, and gained vogue in the hands of negro min-
strels, who, if they touched up the dialogue, never
gave the flavor of cities and theaters to the outdoor
tune. When the itinerant doctor made a stage of his
wagon-top of a Saturday night, it helped the sale of
quack medicines on the village square, and there was
a tapping of feet in the crowd under the torches when
a blackened orchestra set the tune going from fiddle
to fiddle.
    I learned of the myth nearly thirty years ago from
Major G. D. Mercer, who had brought it from the South-
west in the pioneer days and played the tune on the
violin as it should be played to the dialogue.
    First there comes a slow, monotonous sawing of the

notes, which prepares one, as the curtain rises, for
a scene in the backwoods of Arkansas.

The sun is setting over the plains. A belated
horseman in coonskin cap, and well belted with pistol
and bowie-knife, rides up to a squatter cabin to ask
a night's lodging. By the door of a rotting shanty
sits a ragged man astride of a barrel, slowly scraping
out the notes you hear. There are children in the
background, and a slatternly woman stands on the
threshold. The man on the barrel plays away, paying
no attention to the visitor, and the dialogue begins.

"Hello, stranger!" says the horseman.

"Hello yourself!"

"Can you give me a night's lodging?"

"No room, stranger."

The playing goes on.

"Can't you make room?"

"No, sir; it might rain."

"What if it does rain?"

"There's only one dry spot in this house, and me
and Sal sleeps on that."

The playing continues for some time. Then the
horseman asks:

"Which is the way to the Red River Crossing?"

The fiddler gives no answer, and the question is
repeated.

"I've lived hyar twenty years, and never knowed it
to have a crossin'."

The stranger then begins to tease, the tune still
playing.

"Why don't you put a roof on the house?"

"What?"

"Why don't you put a roof on the house?"

"When it's dry I don't want a roof; when it's wet
I can't."

The tune goes on.

"What are you playing that tune over so often for?"

"Only heard it yisterday. 'Fraid I'll forget it."

"Why don't you play the second part of it?"

"I've knowed that tune ten years, and it ain't got no second part."

The crisis of the story has come.

"Give me the fiddle," says the stranger.

The man hands it to him, and a few moments of tuning are needed as a prelude to what follows, which has been immortalized in the popular print here shown, known as "The Turn of the Tune."

When the stranger strikes up, turning away into the unknown second part with the heel-tingling skill of a true jig-player, the whole scene is set in motion. The squatter leaps up, throws out his arms, and begins a dance; the dog wags his tail; the children cut capers; and the "old woman" comes out, twisting her hard face into a smile.

"Walk in, stranger," rings the squatter's voice. "Tie up your horse 'side of ol' Ball. Give him ten ears of corn. Pull out the demijohn and drink it all. Stay as long as you please. If it rains, sleep on the dry spot."

The legend, like all myths, has many variants. Mr. Benham, editor of the Chicago "Arkansas Traveler," and Mr. T. R. Cole of Charleston, West Virginia, have given me versions with more varied dialogues; but the colloquy as to night's lodging, roof, and tune remains about the same, and the student of folk-lore is left to trace its threads of fancy in whatever directions they lead.

I found, to my surprise, the episode of the roof among the memorabilia of York Harbor, Maine, where the legend exists that about 1832 Betty Potter and Esther Booker lived on the dividing line between York and Kittery, in a cabin with a large hole in the roof. One rainy day some ramblers, finding the women boring holes in the floor to let through the drip, asked the following questions and got the following answers:

"Why don't you mend the hole in the roof, Miss

Potter?"

"Can't do it; it rains so."

"Why don't you do it when it don't rain?"

"No need of it then."

"The Arkansas Traveler" is not mentioned among the
border anecdotes in "Beyond the Mississippi," by A. D.
Richardson, nor in Burton's "Cyclopedia of Wit and
Humor," and Professor Child of Harvard told me, when
I wrote to him about it in 1884, that he had made no
study of the ballad-like myth. But it must have traveled to Ireland somewhere in the fifties, as Daniel
Sullivan, a famous fiddler who played it for me at
815 Albany street, Boston, in 1885, had probably
learned it when a young man at Limerick.

There may be many other stories and fiddle tunes
with which it might be compared, though I have heard
only one, called "The Lock Boat after the Scow",
played on the violin, and told me by Mr. George Long
of Doylestown, Pennsylvania, before 1880.

As a canal-boat approaches a lock after dark, the
boatman's tune, played slowly on the fiddle, sounds
above the noise of the sluice and the tinkle of mule-
bells. When the mules have passed, the boat comes
into place as the barefooted lock-boy skips over the
gliding rope. Then the tune stops for the following
dialogue between boatman and boy.

"Got the gate shut behind there?"

"Yes."

"How many laps did you take?"

"Three."

"Are the mules on the tow-path?"

"Yes."

"Are you ready?"

"All ready."

"Let her come."

Then comes the quick turn of the tune to the rush
of the water, while the boat settles quickly down into
the lock. When she rests on the low level the notes

cease for more questions and answers.

"Is the gate open ahead?"

"Yes."

"Is the rope clear of the bridge?"

"All clear."

"Mules on the tow-path?"

"Yes."

"Out of the way, then. Gee-e-ed up!"

And the boat glides away, as she came, to the swinging music.

The farther we travel north the more apt are we to hear the "Arkansas" of the "Traveler" made to rhyme with the word "Matanzas"; but he who feels the true inspiration of the tune sympathizes with the action of the State legislature at Little Rock, which put an end to the "Kansas-ing" of the name in 1881 by making the last syllable rhyme with *raw* and setting the accent on *Ark*; or with Professor William Everett, who stood up and publicly thanked a gentleman for saying "Arkansaw" at a dinner in Washington. There the wish to rhyme it with "Kansas" had been so strong about 1860 that two congressmen from the State had to be addressed by the Speaker of the House as "the gentleman from Arkansas" and "the gentleman from Arkansaw" respectively.

When we seek to trace back the legend to its own country, a surprise is in store for us. To learn from certain authorities in Arkansas that the myth is discountenanced there by a strong State feeling argues ill for our enterprise; and it throws an unexpected seriousness over the situation to be told that the dialogue at the cabin is "a misrepresentation and a slur," and that the hero of the story, pursuing "a strange errand of misconception," has "checked immigration" and "done incalculable injury to the State." To get at the bottom of the matter in a friendly way involves a discussion as to what induces settlers to settle, what people generally do with their ballads

and myths, and what the Californian meant who recently
declared that the demise of Bret Harte would be an
event of the highest possible advantage to California.
All of this produces an atmosphere of solemnity, which,
taking possession of our spirits, might threaten to
become serious, were we not inclined, after mature con-
sideration, to take advantage of the best remedy at
hand, simple but sure. This consists in asking in one
of our old friends to tell the story and to play the
tune.

In the face of these difficulties it is no easy
matter to learn more than that Colonel Sanford C.
Faulkner (born in Scott County, Kentucky, March 3,
1803; died in Little Rock, August 4, 1874) was the
originator of the story, its hero, and in fact the
Arkansas Traveler himself.

Mr. Benham tells me that in the State campaign of
1840, Colonel Faulkner, Hon. A. H. Sevier, Governor
Fulton, Chester Ashley, and Governor Yell, traveling
through the Boston Mountains (Mr. S. H. Newlin, of
"The Arkansas Farmer," Little Rock, says it was Colonel "Sandy" Faulkner and Captain Alber Pike in Yell
County), halted at a squatter's cabin for information.
Colonel "Sandy," who was the spokesman, and no mean
fiddler himself, had some sort of bantering talk with
the squatter, who was sawing at a tune on a violin,
and finally played the second part of it for him.
Out of this, say my informants, grew the "good story"
which the colonel, on his return, was called upon to
tell at a dinner given in the once famous bar-room
near the Anthony House in Little Rock. Years afterward he told it again at a State banquet in New Orleans, when the Governor of Louisiana handed him a
violin and asked him to regale the company with the
then celebrated narrative.

In New Orleans his fame abode with him, for Mr.
Benham adds the curious bit of information that at the
old St. Charles Hotel a special room was devoted to

his use, bearing over the door in gilt letters the
words "The Arkansas Traveler." Mr. N. L. Prentiss,
editor of the Topeka (Kansas) "Commonwealth," says
that Colonel Faulkner's violin was offered for sale in
Little Rock in 1876 for one hundred dollars.

Mr. George E. Dodge of Little Rock wrote me in
1892, in contradiction of most of the above, that the
story of Colonel Faulkner and the squatter was a pure
fiction without a happening-place, "either invented
by Faulkner or by some of his friends, who delighted
in hearing him tell it and play the tune, and made
him the central figure of it more for a joke than
anything else."

But however that might have been, a local artist,
Edward Washburn by name, once living at Dardanelle,
Arkansas, was so much impressed with the story that
he took it into his head, about 1845-50, to paint the
originals. As he then lived with the family of Mr.
Dodge in Little Rock, he made the children pose for
his sketches. Mr. G. E. Doge was the boy in the ash-
hopper, "and we had great times," says he, now fifty
years after, "posing for his figures of the squatter's
children. I was constantly with him in his studio,
and in fact felt that I was helping to paint the picture. The picture representing 'The Turn of the Tune'
was an afterthought. The boy in the ash-hopper gets
down from his perch and takes the stranger's horse.
The children assume different attitudes. But we never
celebrated the completion of the second painting as
we had that of the first. Poor Washburn sickened and
died, and the unfinished work stood upon the easel
until it was stowed away. His executor afterward had
it finished by some one else, and then the two began
to make their appearance in the form of cheap prints."

Another picture, by another painter, which hung in
the Arkansas Building at the Centennial Exhibition at
Philadelphia, had been worked up from photographs of
Mr. Dodge, his brothers and sisters, lent to the

painter by the boy in the ash-hopper.

The tune has a strong flavor of the cottonfield
"hoe-down," but I have obtained no satisfactory information as to its origin. Mr. Benham is sure that
it was not composed by Colonel Faulkner, and has heard,
perhaps to the surprise of musical antiquaries, that
it was either written by Jose Tasso, a famous violin-
player who died in Kentucky some years ago, or produced by him from an old Italian melody. When we come
to investigate this relation of Tasso to "The Arkansas
Traveler" the whole question becomes confused by repeated assertions that Tasso not only composed the
music, but was himself the original of the myth, leaving Faulkner out of the question altogether.

In fact, common opinion on the Ohio River awards
the authorship to Tasso hardly less positively than
on the lower Mississippi the authorship is given ex-
clusively to Faulkner; and it would not be a popular
task to try to convince the "old-timers" of Maysville,
Point Pleasant, and Gallipolis that Faulkner, of whom
they never heard, or any one else except their oft-
quoted favorite, had anything to do with the origin
of the myth. Their recollections make it certain
that Tasso was well known along the river as a con-
cert and dance player when the tune came into vogue.
Robert Clarke, the publisher, heard him play it at
John Walker's brew-house in Cincinnati in 1841 or
1842, and he told Richard R. Reynolds and Albert Crell,
who played with him at a ball at the Burnet House on
New Year's night in 1849, that he himself was the
author of music and story. Mr. Curry, who used to play
the flute to him when he was ill, heard him repeat the
statement about 1850; but Tasso's grandson, Mr. F. G.
Spinning, does not think that his grandfather ever
traveled in Arkansas, and it may be doubted whether
the jocose performer, who from dramatic necessity was
led to make himself the hero of the story, ever claimed
the authorship without winking one eye.

Whether he could equal Faulkner at the dialogue or
not, he seems to have brought down the house with the
tune in a way to outdo all competitors; and one anec-
dote after another connects him with it in the days
of the glory of Mississippi steamboats and when Colt's
revolvers first came down the river. One after another, these tales vouch for a fame so attractive that
the listener is half willing to give up Faulkner and
let Tasso walk off with the honors.

Yet the latter, who spoke broken English until the
day of his death in Covington, Kentucky in 1887, was
born in the city of Mexico, of Italian parents, was
educated in France, and was, it is said, a pupil of
Berlioz; so that it may be questioned whether, even
if, as alleged, he came to Ohio in the thirties, he
could have so steeped himself in the spirit of the
American West as to produce the story. The investi-
gation might lead us much further, but it is doubtful
if more facts gathered about the fable would add to
its interest.

It really matters little where the "Traveler" was
born, whether in Yell County or in the Boston Mountains; whether, as Mr. Dodge asserts, it originated with
Faulkner and his friends, or came from the humor of
Tasso. Like all true creations of fancy, it eludes
definite description and defies criticism, while the
notes of the tune sound a gay disregard of boards of
immigration and State statistics.

The turn of the tune.

«THE ARKANSAS TRAVELER.»
A version arranged for the piano by Mr. P. D. Benham, editor of «The Arkansas Traveler» of Chicago.

BIBLIOGRAPHY

Ferguson, John L., *Arkansas and the Civil War* (Little Rock, 1965)

Randolph, Vance, *The Ozarks* (New York, 1931)

White, Lonnie J., *Politics on the Southwestern Frontier: Arkansas Territory, 1819-1836* (Memphis, 1964)

Wilson, Charles M., *Backwoods America* (Chapel Hill, 1934)

NAME INDEX

NAME INDEX

Adams, John Q., 7
Adams, Samuel, 11
Adkins, Homer M., 26
Ashley, Chester, 11,12

Bailey, Carl E., 24
Bates, Edward, 5
Bates, James W., 5
Baxter, Elisha, 20,21
Benton, Thomas H., 10
Berry, James H., 21
Boles, Thomas, 18
Borland, Solon, 12,13
Bradley, Hugh, 11
Breckinridge, Clifton, 20
Brooks, Joseph, 20
Brough, Charles H., 24
Byrd, Richard C., 12

Calhoun, John, 13
Carraway, Hattie W., 25
Carroll, Charles, 8
Cherry, Francis, 27
Churchill, Thomas J., 21
Clark, William, 3,4
Clarke, James P., 22
Clayton, John M., 20
Clayton, Powell, 18,19
Cleburne, Patrick, 21
Cleveland, Grover, 20,22
Conway, Elias N., 14
Conway, Henry W., 6,7
Conway, James Sevier, 10,13
Craighead, Thomas B., 14
Crawford, William E., 6
Crittenden, Robert, 5,7
Cross, David, 16

Cross, Edward, 10

Dallas, George M., 12
Davis, Jeff, 22
Davis, Jefferson, 16
Davis, Judge, 27
De Soto, Hernando, 1,9
Desha, Benjamin, 10
Donaghey, George W., 23
Drew, Thomas S., 11,12

Eagle, James P., 22
Eisenhower, Dwight D., 27
Elliott, James T., 18

Faubus, Orval E., 27-29
Faulkner, Sanford C., 20
Fishback, William M., 22
Flanagin, Harris, 15,16
Fletcher, Thomas, 16
Franklin, Benjamin, 10
Fulton, William S., 9-11
Futrell, J. M., 23,25

Garland, Augustus H., 20-22
Grant, Ulysses S., 19,21
Greene, Nathaniel, 8
Greenwood, Alfred B., 13

Hadley, Ozro A., 19
Hanks, James M., 19
Harrison, William Henry, 2
Hays, George W., 23
Hempstead, Edward, 4
Hindman, Thomas C., 14,15
Hinds, James, 18
Hinds, Thomas, 5